Special Praise for *The Light Side of the Moon*

"Clinical psychologist Ditta M. Oliker presents the idea that problems and issues that are present in the life of an adult are often the result of hidden beliefs developed by the subconscious self during childhood in order to survive difficult or painful situations.... The theory presented is eye-opening.... This book will help many readers begin to recognize behaviors in their own lives that may stem from a need to protect the child they once were. Dr. Oliker's book is a valuable and unique contribution to the field of psychology."

ForeWord Clarion Review
Five Stars (out of Five)

"In *The Light Side of the Moon*, Dr. Oliker presents a novel way to understand human behavior. She uses a simple Darwinian system to clarify complex psychological phenomena, bringing these events to life through stories of real people and the metaphor of fairytales. The net effect allows us to identify self-defeating patterns and model them. It is a valuable contribution to the literature of psychology."

Allen T. Pack, MD
UCLA Psychiatric Clinical Faculty Association

"Dr. Oliker offers a new understanding of the drama embedded in the demands of our childhood environments that constricts potential. The delight in reading this book is that it presents these constrictions as early adaptations, not pathological stigmas, thus freeing us to become the director of our own lives.

Nancy Illback Cook, PhD
Clinical Psychologist and Adjunct Professor
Baylor College of Medicine

The Light Side of the Moon

The Light Side of the Moon

Reclaiming Your Lost Potential

DITTA M. OLIKER, PhD

CENTRAL RECOVERY PRESS

CENTRAL RECOVERY PRESS

Central Recovery Press (CRP) is committed to publishing exceptional materials addressing addiction treatment, recovery, and behavioral health care topics, including original and quality books, audio/visual communications, and web-based new media. Through a diverse selection of titles, we seek to contribute a broad range of unique resources for professionals, recovering individuals and their families, and the general public.

For more information, visit www.centralrecoverypress.com.

Central Recovery Press, Las Vegas, NV 89129

Publisher: Central Recovery Press
             3321 N. Buffalo Drive
             Las Vegas, NV 89129

17 16 15 14 13 12   1 2 3 4 5

ISBN-13: 978-1-936290-95-6 (trade paper)
ISBN-13: 978-1-937612-03-0 (e-book)

Author photo by Steven Rothfeld. Used with permission.

Material from *The Present Moment in Psychotherapy and Everyday Life* by Daniel Stern, W.W. Norton, Publisher. Used with permission.

Material from *The Mindful Brain: Reflections and Attunement in the Cultivation of Well-Being* by Daniel J. Siegel, W.W. Norton, Publisher. Used with permission.

"Intrude," "invade," "echo," definitions. Used by permission. From Merriam-Webster's Collegiate® Dictionary, 11th Edition © 2012 by Merriam-Webster, Incorporated (www.Merriam-Webster.com).

Anaïs Nin quoted by permission, granted by Tree L. Wright, Author's Representative. Copyright the Anaïs Nin Trust. All rights reserved.

Publisher's Note: This book contains general information about human development; it is not medical advice, and should not be treated as such. Central Recovery Press makes no representations or warranties in relation to the information herein; this book is not an alternative to medical advice from your doctor or other professional healthcare provider.

Our books represent the experiences and opinions of their authors only. Every effort has been made to ensure that events, institutions, and statistics presented in our books as facts are accurate and up-to-date. To protect their privacy, some of the names of people and institutions have been changed.

Cover design by Deb Tremper, Six Penny Graphics
Interior design and layout by Deb Tremper, Six Penny Graphics

To all of my patients whose journeys to the light side of their moon showed me the power of reclaiming lost potential, and whose stories, struggles, and successes fill these pages.

CONTENTS

PART TWO

The Three Basic Elements of a Survival System

PART THREE

Breaking Free from a Survival System

PREFACE

A Moon Story

THE BEGINNING OF MY PERSONAL JOURNEY

Steve, the eldest of my three sons, was the child who first asked, and then demanded, answers to The Questions. Whenever I saw him furrowing his brow in a particular way, a Big Question was sure to follow. I was anticipating one about where babies come from and had read some material in order to be fully prepared.

On this particular day Steve, now seven years old, came into the kitchen with a Big Question all over his face. I waited, smug in the knowledge that I was capable of dealing with such weighty matters as to how the sperm gets in, what body parts are involved, how the baby gets out, and what happens in-between. He paused a moment and then said, "My teacher wasn't in school today. Her husband died. What does it mean when someone dies?" I felt trapped. What do you say to a child to explain death?

"Death is like going to sleep," my mother had said in answer to my childish inquiry. I remembered my own fear when my eyes would start to close at night and did not want to pass that fear on to my child. So I evaded Steve's question by diverting his attention. Of course I knew that he would ask me again.

And two weeks later he did. "Well," I said, "life and death are like the moon. The moon has a light side, which we can see, and a dark side that is always hidden but that we know to be there. These two parts, the one we can see and the other that we can't, are really part of a whole. One side of the moon can't exist without the other. If you think of it that way, life and death are also part of a whole. We can't have one without the other. And after a long, full life, death is like the dark side of the moon." My answer seemed to satisfy his curiosity.

Years later, in February of 1973, I answered a call from the sheriff's department in Santa Cruz, California. They informed me that my second son, David, then 18 years old, who had been camping with friends in the local mountains, was a victim of a mass killing. "I'm sorry to tell you, ma'am," the officer had said, "those four boys in the tent hadn't a chance against a loaded rifle."

In all, thirteen people were shot by a young man recently released from a psychiatric hospital. There are no adequate words to describe my feelings. I was drowning in sorrow and grief; David was dead and I too was dying.

One night, several months after that devastating phone call and unable again to sleep, I prowled around my house looking for something, anything, to ease my agitation. Through the window, my eye was caught by the brilliance of a full moon. I stood there staring at the moon and began to feel a stirring of an elusive memory. Of course! I remembered Steve's question about what it means to die. What was it I answered, so long ago? That life and death were like the light and dark sides of the moon. I knew then that I was on the dark side of the moon. The death of my son was also the death of a part of me. My first response to remembering was one of anger and disgust. How could I have given such a superficial, meaningless answer as an explanation for life's greatest trauma? But as I stood looking at the moon, the meaning of that story took on a new, healing urgency. If death and life are part of a whole and I am now on the dark side of the moon, then somewhere there must exist a light side—a life side—of the moon.

I spoke to the moon, as if it were my lost son. "I will always mourn your death, David, but to celebrate your life, I must not waste my life. There has been far too much waste already."

I stood at that window through the night watching the moon make its way across the sky and took the first tentative steps in my long journey back to its light side. I knew that night that somehow I would find my way and survive.

My journey took me to and through places I would never have imagined, including enrollment in a doctoral program in psychology. I believe my move toward psychology offered a necessary and hoped-for healing change in my life. The world of theater in which I had existed for many years was no longer real enough for me. Having been on the dark side of the moon, I now needed to live in a different kind of reality; by becoming someone in a position to help others, I was allowing myself an opportunity to deal with the horrible sense of waste that had permeated my world. The lessons learned, the insights gained, and my personal understanding of human behavior, are all part of that life-affirming journey. In struggling for my own survival I developed an invaluable appreciation for the survival struggle of others.

My purpose in writing *The Light Side of the Moon* is to share what I have learned about why the life we want, and the potential to have it, is denied us. This book is about recovering the inherent joy and power of life. The stories it tells, real and symbolic, may offer some guidance to your finding the light side of your moon.

ACKNOWLEDGMENTS

This book took form over a number of years, and innumerable discussions, letters, and emails with friends and colleagues who offered encouragement, suggestions, critiques, and guidance. To all of you, my heartfelt thanks and gratitude for: your interest in the project; your insight into maximizing the psychological value of each story; and, most importantly, your support and recognition of the possibilities of change in my concept of survival systems—a concept rooted in the works of Charles Darwin and D.W. Winnicott.

This book owes its authenticity to the eight personal histories that form its core. I am deeply appreciative of the individuals who had the willingness to allow me to tell their life stories. In several cases, they even suggested the name of the character in their story. These are true stories, modified only to protect the privacy of the individual.

This book would not have been written or published were it not for the crucial involvement of both of my sons, Steve and Bob Oliker. They have acted as the stewards and guardians of the book, from their earliest belief in me and their encouragement of my work. They have been by my side every step of the way as this book took form, including their active participation in the editing and publishing process. There are no words that can fully express my feelings of gratitude for the difference they have made in my being able to claim my potential as a writer and as a psychologist who can hopefully make a difference in the lives of you, the readers.

PART ONE

The Opponent Within and How It Came to Be You

CHAPTER ONE

Unhappily Ever After

You know what you want but you can't seem to get it. Could it be you have a hidden need to not get what you want?

Some people seek ways of changing chronic self-defeating behaviors that limit their success and their quality of life. But even as they express their sincere desire to change—repeatedly attempt to change—real change remains hidden and unattainable as they continue to sabotage any of their attempts to change. "I want to get that promotion," he says—but he is consistently late to important meetings. "I want to get married and have children," she says—but she consistently picks unavailable men. "I want to express my ideas," he says—but given the chance, he has nothing to say.

The Light Side of the Moon: Reclaiming Your Lost Potential makes sense of these seemingly irrational and resistant behaviors and proposes that they represent survival adaptations to the early environment of childhood, originally serving as legitimate responses to threats and potential dangers in the physical and psychological environment of that childhood. Established in childhood and rooted in a child's belief of how to survive, these adaptive responses continue to operate silently and unseen, becoming the persistent, defeating behaviors of adulthood—the hidden opponents within that block inherent potential. I call these adaptive responses "survival systems" because they are patterns of behaviors, attitudes and beliefs that originally functioned to maintain a sense of safety.

A crucial idea in this book is that an individual exists, a "you" who is separate and unlike any other. A "you" born with a unique set of characteristics, physical attributes, talents, abilities, and inherent potential—with a promise of fulfilling this potential. What do you do when this inherent "you" is far below your potential and not getting what you want? Like many people caught in this dilemma, you start searching for answers that will tell you how to change that which you seem to be unable to change. You sign up for classes that offer information on how to achieve one's goals—but you stay stuck in inactivity. You read one self-help book after another—but your "new you" disappears after awhile. You try psychotherapy—but find that the core reasons for your self-defeating behaviors elude both you and the therapist. Eventually you may come to believe that your chronic inability to change must mean that there is something intrinsically wrong with you. You are, at this point, not unlike many of the individuals with whom I have worked as a psychotherapist. It is at this point that it is time for you to start asking: *"Is it possible that I am caught in a survival system and that, as a child, I had to develop a hidden need to not get what I want?"*

At first the question seems simplistic, but raising the possibility of a powerful unknown need to be unable to change modifies the perspective on behavior and opens new doors to possible explanations. The paradox is that once you acknowledge that you can't change, you are free, perhaps for the first time, to start changing.

The concept of a survival system is based on a loose interpretation of Darwinian ideas. According to his theory, a species adapts and accommodates to its environment in order to survive. This book proposes that—what is true for a species in the physical world is also true for a given individual in his or her psychological world. Thus, understanding the difference between "want to" and "need to" is crucial in your changing your survival system. A "want to" is a goal-oriented change in a behavior, belief, or attitude that represents what you, as an adult, believe you are capable of achieving. As used in this book, "need to" refers to the behavior, belief, or attitude that represents what you, as a child, believed you needed to be or do—or not to be or do—in order to continue to safely exist in the environment of your childhood. "Need to" becomes synonymous with survival.

The Light Side of the Moon: Reclaiming Your Lost Potential uses case histories, theoretical approaches, and the findings of various research inquiries to offer the reader a broad understanding of the meaning and power of a survival system.

Breaking free from a survival system means that you break free of fear based on behavior that no longer has relevance in your life. It begins when you loosen the grip of the past, a past that has kept you a prisoner of your childhood. A starting point is the recognition that there is a crucial difference between a pattern of behavior that is a direct result of *experiencing* a trauma and one that is the result of trying to *avoid* a trauma. In simplistic terms, it is the difference between taking a direct hit by a flying object or ducking to avoid that object. The direct hit is a trauma to the body, causing pain and an observable injury. The act of ducking avoids the trauma and, when used appropriately, can be a positive move. But the act of ducking, when it becomes a generalized reaction to the possibility—or imagined possibility—of being hit, can also have serious consequences. Consistent physical, psychological, and emotional "ducking" in childhood can lead to a pattern of behaviors that eventually cause pain and a hidden diminution of inherent potential.

Working with patients unable to change, I discovered a way to help them understand the difference between the effects of "taking a direct hit" and the hidden long-term damage of "ducking."

Because fairy tales are universally known, I use them as metaphors to convey the meaning of survival systems and how they represent safety to a child. A most compelling tale for this purpose is "Snow White and the Seven Dwarfs," collected by the Brothers Grimm, because the story revolves around a young girl's struggle to survive a dangerous childhood. I tell my patients two versions in order to highlight how children can either *react* or *adapt* to their environment.

Three Versions of a Fairy Tale

The first version, "Snow White: A Tale of Reaction," relates what would happen to a young child who experienced a series of traumas. The second, "Snow White: A Tale of Survival," represents what many of us, as children, believed we needed to do or be in order to avoid experiencing a trauma. We then unknowingly take these beliefs, in the form of survival systems, into adulthood. An internalized need to survive the dangers of childhood is stronger than the desire to thrive as an adult. If we had believed that being pretty would kill us, we would be ugly. If we had thought there was danger in speaking out, we would be silent. If we had sensed success would deprive us of parental involvement, we would fail.

I like to review the original fairy tale because many people exposed to the more romanticized version by Disney and others may not be familiar with all of the dangers the young heroine experienced.

Snow White: The Original Fairy Tale

In the original fable, a queen wishes for a beautiful child, and her wish is answered with the birth of Snow White. The Queen dies when the child is born, and within a year, the King remarries. His beautiful new wife is vain and cannot bear that anyone be lovelier than she. The new Queen has a magic mirror and each time she asks:

> *"Mirror, mirror on the wall,*
> *Who is fairest of us all?"*

The mirror answers:

> *"Queen, thou art the fairest of us all."*

The Queen is pleased, for she knows the mirror does not lie.

As the years pass, Snow White grows more beautiful and when she is only seven years old, the Queen is surprised when the mirror responds with:

> *"Queen, thou art the fairest in this hall,*
> *But Snow White's fairer than us all."*

Horrified, the Queen grows green with envy. From that moment she is consumed with rage and hatred. Finally she calls a huntsman and orders him to take the child out into the forest. "I don't want to lay eyes on her again," she tells him. "Kill her and bring me her heart as a token."

The hunter takes pity on Snow White but also assumes that the wild beasts of the forest will eat her. He lets her go and brings back an animal's heart to placate the Queen. Snow White wanders for hours. At last she finds a little house owned by seven dwarfs, and they invite Snow White to stay with them. She, in turn, offers to cook and clean for them while they go off to the mountain each day to dig for gold.

True to her narcissistic nature, the wicked Queen soon consults her magic mirror and discovers that Snow White is still alive. This time, the Queen determines to kill the child herself. Disguised as a peddler, she sells Snow White some colorful laces and offers to lace Snow White's bodice. But she ties the strings so tightly that the young girl loses her breath. The dwarfs return that evening, discover Snow White on the ground, and cut the tight laces. Snow White begins to breathe again.

In her second attempt, the Queen, disguised again, gives Snow White a poisoned comb. As soon as the comb is in her hair, Snow White falls senseless to the ground. The dwarfs remove the comb and once more save her.

More determined than ever, the Queen returns for the third time, now disguised as a feeble old woman. She offers Snow White an apple, half of which has been dipped in poison. The Queen cuts the apple in half, eats the safe side, and convinces the now-wary girl to take a bite of the poisoned half. The moment Snow White does, she slumps to the ground.

Again the dwarfs return to find Snow White seemingly lifeless, but this time they cannot revive her. She looks so beautiful that they decide to encase her in a glass coffin in which she continues to sleep for many years.

One day, a prince happens to stop by the dwarfs' house, sees the glass coffin, and falls in love with Snow White. He begs the dwarfs to let him take her to his castle and they agree. While carrying the glass coffin, the prince's servants slip and drop it. With the shock of the fall, the poisoned piece of apple that Snow

White had bitten off comes out of her throat and she awakens. The overjoyed prince asks Snow White to marry him and invites the entire kingdom—including the wicked Queen—to their wedding. Consumed with envy of Snow White's beauty, the Queen dances herself to death. Snow White and her prince live happily ever after.

Snow White: A Tale of Reaction

I call my first adaptation of the Snow White story "A Tale of Reaction" to illustrate what happens to the young heroine when her story is transposed to a world of psychological reality. The comments, in italics, are what a child taking a direct hit would experience in reaction to each event.

A Queen wishes for a beautiful child—she dies when the child is born—and the King remarries. [*The loss of a mother and a father's remarriage are major traumas. The king is nowhere to be found in the story and his absence would contribute to the child's feelings of abandonment.*] The new Queen needs to be "the fairest of all" and confirms that with her questioning of the magic mirror.

As the years pass, Snow White grows more beautiful. When she is seven years old [*still very much a child*] the mirror surprises the Queen by replying that "Snow White's fairer than us all."

Horrified, the Queen grows green with envy. [*Envy conveys a destructive impulse. It is not only that someone wants what you have but also implies that you will be destroyed for having it.*] The Queen, consumed with rage, orders a huntsman to kill the child.

The hunter, feeling pity, lets Snow White go. [*The huntsman's failure to protect the child and his need to placate the Queen at Snow White's expense leads to even deeper feelings of distrust and abandonment.*]

Snow White finds the dwarfs' house and is invited to stay. She offers to cook and clean for them. [*Only seven years old, she assumes adult responsibilities. A child forced into pseudo-adulthood can experience undue pressure and increased anxiety.*]

The wicked Queen, discovering the child still alive, disguises herself as a peddler, sells Snow White some laces for her bodice, and ties them too tightly. [*This murderous attempt makes Snow White fearful of peddlers, laces, and asphyxiation, and reinforces her difficulty in trusting others.*]

Next the Queen gives Snow White a poisoned comb. As soon as it is in her hair, Snow White falls senseless to the ground. [*Now Snow White will fear the receipt of gifts, the loss of consciousness, and the arrival of strangers.*] The dwarfs remove the comb and once more save her. [*The dwarfs have now twice saved her but do not offer to protect her. A child would feel terribly alone and vulnerable.*]

The Queen returns for the third time. Now disguised as an old woman, she offers Snow White an apple and convinces the now-wary girl to take a bite of the poisoned half. The moment Snow White does, she slumps to the ground. [*This last trickery destroys Snow White's ability to trust even her own judgment.*]

Again the dwarfs return, but this time cannot revive her. They encase her in a glass coffin in which she sleeps for many years, without aging.

One day, a Prince stops by and falls in love with Snow White. The coffin drops, the poisoned apple comes out of her throat, and she awakens. [*Awakening in a coffin would be a traumatic experience for anyone.*] Overjoyed, the prince asks Snow White to marry him.

Unfortunately, Snow White cannot take advantage of her good fortune. Although the Prince loves her and gives her whatever she desires, she has been severely damaged by her experiences. Her debilitating anxiety disorder is exhibited by phobic reactions to laces, combs, apples, coffins, and old ladies. She suffers from insomnia and sleep deprivation because she is afraid of losing consciousness, and her increasing panic at the sight of strangers means she must limit her world to her room in the castle. She was recently diagnosed as suffering a severe post-traumatic stress disorder. The Prince has been patient but is getting discouraged with Snow White's fears that he will abandon her and with her overwhelming distrust of one and all. The good Prince is losing faith that he and his bride can live happily ever after.

Snow White: A Tale of Survival

My second version, called "A Tale of Survival," illustrates how a child might adapt in order to avoid the potential traumas in her life. This story captures the essence of a survival system.

The story begins the same way, but sometime before her seventh birthday, this Snow White senses a threat. Having suffered several major traumas, including the death of her mother, abandonment by her father, and the growing negative vibrations of her stepmother, she has become acutely sensitive to the dangers around her.

As a child, Snow White cannot intellectually grasp the idea that the adults in her world are dysfunctional and dangerous. But she has witnessed the Queen's reactions to a particularly ornate mirror and, in powerful intuitive ways, senses that she is not safe and can trust no one. She recognizes that she will have to save herself and knows, *without conscious awareness*, that there is danger in that mirror.

"How do I stay out of that mirror?" Her non-conscious survival self asks. Thinking in a concrete and literal way, as children do, she answers her own question with: "If I am ugly, the mirror will not say I am the fairest of them all." And to make sure she avoids her stepmother's envy, Snow White will believe that the Queen is indeed the fairest of them all.

Snow White develops a "being ugly" survival system that takes precedence over everything else. She consumes large quantities of food, adding many pounds to her once-normal size. As she matures, she maintains her extra weight regardless of how many diets she attempts. She wears clothes that are unflattering, inappropriate, and either too big or too small. Her face bears the brunt of her picking and scratching, her skin is the victim of neglect, and her stringy hair defies all attempts at styling. To sum it up, she looks unattractive, unkempt, and unhappy.

Her friends say, "Snow White, you could be so pretty. You have such lovely features. If you would just lose some weight and dress differently and . . ."

Snow White, who doesn't consciously want to be ugly, responds eagerly to all suggestions. She goes from one diet to another, from one beauty salon to another, from one stylist to another, but nothing works. Outsiders see her as undisciplined, and her friends grow tired of her promises and complaints. Self-consciousness about her appearance affects Snow White's sense of self-esteem and, as the years go by, she becomes more withdrawn and unhappy.

The Queen takes pity on this ugly Snow White and treats her as if she were her own daughter. Although the young woman feels safe with her stepmother, the emptiness in her life and her inability to attract a partner convince her that she will live unhappily ever after.

In "A Tale of Reaction" the heroine has taken a direct hit from the stepmother's narcissism and envy. The adult Snow White's suffering is severe but understandable, given all she has experienced. If help were available, she would be given medication and psychiatric support and, hopefully, be able to function somewhat normally.

The Snow White in "A Tale of Survival" ducked and developed a survival system that guaranteed she would not become beautiful, thus keeping her potential below the radar of the stepmother's envy. Those adaptive patterns continued into her adulthood even though the stepmother was no longer such a serious threat. This Snow White is less obviously damaged and so she is treated less sympathetically. No one knows about the magic mirror or the stepmother's hidden envy. Don't forget, as long as Snow White stays "ugly," she does not activate the stepmother's—*or anyone else's*—envy and rage. No one, including this adult Snow White, recognizes the awesome power of her internalized system of survival, which may have kept her alive but is now keeping her from change and growth.

My first version, "Snow White: A Tale of Reaction," deals with what happens to Snow White after she appears in the mirror. But when possible, children adapt so they can avoid getting caught in a mirror. "Magic mirrors" are dangerous and frightening, and once caught in them, the child may have to depend on others. But in a world of difficult or uncaring adults, that dependence can be as dangerous as a magic mirror. The child can't afford the risk and so the survival system of the child is indelibly stamped in the avoidant mechanisms of the adult.

It is this understanding of the hidden need to adapt that underlies the basis for *The Light Side of the Moon: Reclaiming Your Lost Potential*. In the next story of Beth, and in all the stories that follow, you will find illustrations of how the demands of an archaic and obsolete survival system determined what the child needed to be or do, rather than what the child's potential would have allowed him or her to be or do.

The process of change is not easy. It begins with an understanding of why you have been unable to change—of why you may have needed *not* to change. It requires recognizing what you—as a child—believed you needed to do—or not do—in order to survive. This recognition must be followed by your taking the necessary steps to alter your behavior, as an adult, in ways that free you from the tyranny of an archaic survival system, no longer necessary or appropriate.

Join me now in a journey to discover the hidden reasons why you have been unable to become who it is you want to be and achieve what it is you want to gain.

CHAPTER TWO

Happily Ever After

I have found that an effective way to help my patients is by sharing someone else's story, particularly more difficult cases that offer the most insight and understanding. Hearing how and why someone else was blocked and the steps he or she took to break free offers clues to uncovering one's own survival system. Case histories help break through feelings of isolation by allowing identification with someone caught in a similar adaptive pattern. Each story in this book—based on patients with whom I have worked—describes a different reason for adaptation, the behaviors and beliefs the adaptation required, the process the person went through in uncovering the system of survival, and the changes made to break free.

One of the case histories bears an uncanny resemblance to "Snow White: A Tale of Survival."

The Need to Be Ugly: Beth

"Just look at me," Beth said. "I'm disgustingly overweight and nothing seems to help. I'm only twenty-seven and I look like I'm forty. It's not fair. Men don't seem to know that I'm alive."

This was Beth at our first meeting. Looking at her, I could understand why she felt that way. She was perhaps fifty pounds too heavy and dressed in clothes that were formless, matronly, and hanging loosely enough to allow her to hide within them. Her short, blond hair, cropped in an unflattering style, seemed to accentuate the pudginess of her face. Her lightly colored lips betrayed her only use of makeup. A friend had suggested that she see a therapist about her weight problem.

Beth's history sounded benign. Her father was a successful doctor, her mother a homemaker, and she had an older brother and two younger sisters. Although Beth saw her mother as somewhat anxious—"My mother might be taking a bit too many prescription drugs"—she believed that in general they'd been the typical TV suburban family, dog and all.

Beth had not been heavy as a child. A good student, she spent the year after college graduation overseas where she'd worked as an English-language instructor. At that time she had thought that she would work toward completing a doctorate in English literature.

Returning to California, she began to explore various graduate programs but found that her mother, who now worked in the father's office, was scheduled for surgery. Beth offered to fill in until her mother was well again. At the time of starting therapy, she had been on her father's staff for five years. Her mother, long since recovered, had never returned to work.

"I really should look for a new job," Beth would say. "Working for my father is not what I had in mind when I came back from Europe."

I'd ask her what she would prefer to do.

"I'd get into a graduate program," she'd say, "or maybe finish my credentials and get a job as a teacher."

Invariably she would find reasons why the time wasn't right. I began to wonder if Beth had a hidden need to not find another job, if somehow her resistance to change represented a survival system. But then, there could be other reasons for her being stuck, including low self-esteem, fear of growing up, or possibly laziness.

Beth had male friends in high school and college but little one-to-one experience with men. "I preferred," she said, "to be part of the group." Translated, that meant that she had not dated during her school years and felt the loss of not having had a boyfriend. She'd had a brief relationship two years prior to our first meeting, but the romance lasted only a short time and had ended in disappointment. Her eyes filled with tears as she said, "He was only using me to make his last girlfriend jealous." Heartbroken when he became engaged to the other girl, she began to worry that she might be unmarriageable.

The issue of her marriageability soon took precedence. Her struggle with weight loss seemed tied to the question of marriage, for she believed that the former was a necessary condition of the latter. I did not understand, at that time, what marriage meant to her, but it did seem to be the "unreachable dream." In pursuit of that dream, Beth had joined an orthodox religious community that was rooted in tradition, patriarchal in its functioning, and family-oriented. The community required that its members live in a prescribed area and encouraged them to stay within the community, physically and socially. Beth had recently moved into an apartment purchased by her parents within the geographic boundaries of the community. At the time of our early meetings, Beth felt that she belonged in the group and that she would realize her dream of marrying and having a large family of her own.

Meanwhile, another picture began to emerge from Beth's memories. The family, it seemed, was not as secure as she had remembered. Her father's medical education had been partially supported by the Army Reserves; and when Beth was seven years old, he had been sent to Vietnam. Her mother, she reported, had been overwhelmed by the possibility of his being wounded or killed. As the eldest daughter and the "responsible" child, she assumed the role abdicated by her mother, an act she repeated years later when she took her mother's place on her father's staff. To further confuse the family dynamics, her mother was hooked on tranquilizers, with Beth's father the likely supplier. Beth's siblings were married or pursuing careers, leaving her the only one still involved in the parents' lives.

By now I was convinced that a survival system existed but had difficulty grasping its purpose. My focus was on Beth's mother since it seemed that she would be most affected by any changes her daughter made. We now spent hours untangling the strands of Beth's discontent, trying to find why and when she'd gotten stuck. It was clear that she wanted a different life.

"I don't want to be an old maid," she'd say. "I want a meaningful job that pays me what I'm worth. And I want to lose weight!"

I'd ask if she had permission to lose weight, thinking that her mother might be threatened by Beth's becoming attractive. My musings about permission only angered her. "You keep harping on the same theme," she'd complain. "Of course I have permission to lose weight. It's just that my damn body won't cooperate."

I wondered if her body wasn't actually cooperating all too well, but with another imperative.

In the months that followed, Beth grappled with the tension of her two warring parts. One wanted to be married, have children, and enjoy a profession. The other part was stuck living a monastic life, caught in a rigid patriarchal community, and still working for daddy. Her attempts to lose weight invariably failed, and she remained heavy and matronly. She was also directly or indirectly expressing anger and frustration with me. She would "forget" to come to a session or, at the last moment, find some task she had to attend to. My interpretations of her resistance only caused more resistance. I began to find her difficult.

"There must be something wrong with me," she'd say. "It's not normal to not be able to change. And I'm desperate to be free."

"Yes," I'd answer, "but free from what?"

There seemed to be no answer to that question. Perhaps I was mistaken in my evaluation of her. Perhaps she was not caught in a survival system, but in a dynamic that was beyond my understanding. I sought consultation for myself in trying to help her. And when she finally raised the question of seeing a therapist who was a member of her community, I must confess, I felt relieved. It is difficult to feel the pain of another human being week after week and be unable to help.

Four months later Beth returned, and I cannot say I was thrilled to see her. Beth's objections to some of the group's beliefs had created friction with the other therapist and she decided to re-connect with me. By this time we had been meeting for a year and a half and she was more depressed than ever. I recommended she consult a psychiatrist for anti-depressants.

"Absolutely not," she shot back. "My father is still angry at me for going to a shrink that he doesn't know and didn't recommend. He would have a fit if he found out I'm on drugs."

I asked her if I could speak to him about his objections. She agreed and I called her father. We had a long conversation in which I expressed my concern for the depth of her depression and told him, truthfully, that she had expressed suicidal thoughts that would be dangerous to ignore. I also told him that Beth had refused any medication because of what he would say and that it would be helpful if he could encourage her. I believed that we had had a useful conversation and that he understood the seriousness of the situation.

The next time Beth came to my office, she handed me a yellow envelope. "I think you had better have these pills my father gave me," she said. "He said you thought I should be on antidepressants. I don't trust myself to have them and I'm a little surprised he gave them to me."

It was more than surprising, for he had given her a dose that could be lethal. Beth's giving me the envelope represented the part of her that was healthy. For me, it was confirmation that Beth was trapped in a survival system and a major clue that her father was not only overly involved in her life, but was dangerous as well.

I did refer Beth to a psychiatrist and at first the medication seemed to help. But soon she was caught in the same depressive cycle. Each time I tried to explore why her father would risk giving her so many pills, she would find an excuse. "He must have misunderstood you," she'd say, or "He probably thought that you meant he should prescribe them." My rebuttals to her excuses for her father's behavior didn't make a dent in her wall of resistance.

No matter what Beth attempted to do—lose weight, get a new job, even change her hairstyle—nothing changed. She was sinking into a more serious depression. Statements like "I so wanted to have children," combined with signs of hopelessness—deep sighs, the defeated slump of her shoulders—told me I was witnessing a soul in such pain that life was becoming unlivable. I had seen her in the morning and our session nagged at me the rest of that hot, August day.

"What's the use?" she had asked. "Nothing is ever going to change. Maybe I don't want it to change and this is the way it's supposed to be."

"No," I answered, "it isn't the way it's supposed to be. You have a life ahead of you that's worth fighting for."

"Maybe you're right," she said, but there didn't seem to be much fight left in her.

The more I thought about her, the more I believed that Beth was approaching a suicide attempt. I tried to reach her throughout the day and I could feel myself getting more anxious with each unanswered call. Finally, at about ten o'clock that night, she answered the phone.

I told her that I had been uneasy about our session and wanted to make sure she was all right. As we talked, I felt an increasing tension in the pit of my stomach and knew that I had to confront her.

"You're planning to kill yourself, aren't you?" I said.

"Yes," she answered, "and there's no way you can stop me. I'm leaving right now and you won't know where I'm going."

"Beth, listen to me. Suicide is the ultimate solution. There's no deciding later to change your mind. Give yourself more time. You can always kill yourself tomorrow."

"That's what I'm planning to do," she said.

"What do you mean?" I said, surprised by her answer.

"I'm planning to kill myself tomorrow," she repeated

"Tomorrow! Why tomorrow?" This made no sense.

"It's a special religious holiday and the one day when I can kill myself with God's blessing."

She explained her interpretation of how, on this day—and this one day only—God would not condemn her if she took her own life. The fact that her religion did not condone suicide was not important at that moment. What mattered was that she had convinced herself that she had God's permission to kill herself, and she was determined. Nothing could stop her, and that is what she told me.

I wish I could say I am clever enough to have planned what I said next, but it was the first thing that came to mind—and the truth.

"But you can't kill yourself tomorrow," I implored. "Tomorrow's my birthday."

"Your birthday!" She paused. "Is it really your birthday?" I could hear the doubt in her voice.

"Yes, it really is," I answered. "I'll show you my driver's license."

There was a long silence and then she started to cry. "No," she said at last, "I can't do this to you. I can't ruin your birthday for the rest of your life."

I saw Beth the next day. The black cloud that had enveloped her was gone, and I sensed that she had experienced a major breakthrough and shift in her survival system. I asked Beth to help me understand how she had experienced our interaction and why it had made such a profound difference.

"As I told you last night," she explained, "I truly believed that I had permission from God to take my life today, but only today. But then you said that today was your birthday, and that changed everything. To me that's God's sign that He means me to live. I can't explain just why, but I feel that I've been freed from something that has kept me trapped all of my life."

I saw Beth's breakthrough as a result of her powerful belief that God had commanded her to live, and that His power was greater than the power that had imprisoned her. As she later said, "It could not have been an accident that of the 365 days in the year, that one was your birthday."

Beth's first action after this shift was to leave her father's office and take a job involving motivational work for a national weight-reducing company. In less than a year, she lost most of her excess weight, becoming not only one of the company's best advertisements, but also one of its top managers. Heavy, matronly Beth was transformed into the young woman who now arrived at my office, smartly dressed, attractive, with long, wavy hair, and a size eight figure. She was thrilled one day when she reported that someone had called her "sexy."

Her physical transformations were matched by the changes in her behavior and lifestyle. She began by confronting the leader of her religious community, a man who, she believed, placed his interests ahead of the group members. Minor confrontations led to a major disagreement, and Beth knew she had to leave the group. Beth's leaving the security of the community was a prelude to her breaking the strings that bound her to her family. She began by moving out of the apartment owned by her parents. For the first time in many years, she, and she alone, decided where she wanted to live.

"I think I'm in big trouble," Beth said one day. "I thought my family would calm down and not be so critical of me. But they haven't, and I can't help feeling guilty. My mother seems so overworked, and it's obvious that my father feels betrayed. And I feel like I'm turning into an awful, selfish person."

I reminded her of the power of a survival system and how her changing could be threatening to the family members.

The reasons for Beth's hidden need to be ugly began to openly play out. Both parents, but particularly her father, were upset by her growing independence. She was now earning a reasonable salary and was choosing not to be financially dependent on them. Her siblings echoed the parental disapproval, and family gatherings became a time to "set Beth straight." Although she had begun to recognize that her family suffered from too much togetherness, reinforced by father's financial "generosity," she was still struggling to understand the key role she played and why her pulling away was sending shock waves through the family's structure.

"I've never been so alone," Beth said one day as the family's counter-offensive increased. "I feel as if I'm out there in space, in the darkness, not connected to anything solid. And I'm scared because I'm not sure I'm going to make it." And although she was verbalizing her feelings of isolation vis à vis her family, in reality, she was beginning to form new attachments and develop new relationships, which were still in their nascent stages, which accounted for her tenuous and fearful lack of confidence.

"It's like being a performer on a trapeze," I reassured her. "There's that moment when you let go of one trapeze bar to grab another. That's exactly where you are now. You've let go of your family—but you haven't quite grabbed the other bar, which is your new life. That's what it feels like to break a survival system. It's like being up near the top of the tent, suspended in space, with no safety net."

Beth made her leap and caught the hands of the man who turned out to be her "Prince Charming." All the old fears of not being marriageable faded; and, after a short courtship, her "Prince" asked her to marry him. Did they play out the fairy tale and live happily ever after? So far they have, but some of the other characters in the story did not fare so well.

The answer to why Beth had needed to be ugly was more fully revealed during her wedding celebration. Her father's rude behavior and angry words revealed his fury at being abandoned by his daughter. The idea that Beth now "belonged" to another man was intolerable, and he openly expressed his rage.

Beth was finally able to understand that she had developed her "need to be ugly" survival system because being ugly was synonymous with being unmarriageable, and being unmarriageable meant that she would remain in the role assigned to her since childhood. Beth's mother, struggling with her own insecurities and dependent on tranquilizers, had been unable to function effectively, resulting in her becoming an anxious and seemingly "fragile" woman. Beth, the eldest girl and temperamentally suited to the task, had become the primary maternal figure, the facilitator, the interpreter, the conduit through which the family communicated. She was the linchpin that held them together—a shadow wife—a shadow mother. In order to remain totally available to the family of her birth, Beth could not have a family of her own.

Freed of the burden of her survival system of needing to be ugly, Beth was finally free to live her own life. And every year in the hot days of August, I receive a special birthday card.

CHAPTER THREE

Understanding Your "Need To"

Asking a person if he or she has a <u>need to not change</u> often elicits a dismissive reaction, as if the question is too simplistic to be taken seriously. The question itself may be simple, but the answer includes theories and research findings that explore and define the complexity of the environment of childhood as well as the factors that drive a need for a survival system. Included in the material of this chapter is a basic review of Darwin's theory of natural selection, a brief review of recent neuroscience studies that have significance for understanding the nature of "knowing," the power of attachment, an exploration of whose needs got met, and how children understand their world.

Some of the material in this and later chapters may appear, at first, to be unnecessarily technical or academic and may indeed require more than one reading. But don't be put off by these chapters, for the information found in them will not only offer you a better understanding of the significance of the case histories but, more importantly, greater insight into your personal history.

The Evolution of Your Survival System

Understanding "need to" takes us first to Charles Darwin and his theory of natural selection, a theory grounded in concepts of survival. Plants and animals survive, according to Darwin, because they adapt to their environment by utilizing two primary patterns. The first pattern is *conformity to the demands of an environment*, which means that the species exists in harmony with the specific requirements of its environment. For example, think of the differences between the foliage in an equatorial rain forest and that found in a colder, arid territory. In the rain forest, foliage is dense and water is plentiful. We find that plants, in order to maximize the absorption of rainfall, have roots that lie closer to the surface and fan out in order to cover a greater surface area. In an arid climate, there is less competition but also less water. Therefore, plants have deep roots in order to tap into a more permanent source of water and stalks capable of storing water.

Achieving this conformity to the demands of an environment is accomplished through *innovation* and *adaptation*. Innovation is the introduction of something new, and adaptation refers to an ability to adjust or modify. A good example of Darwinian innovation/adaptation is a snowshoe hare, which changes its coloration from white in the winter to reddish brown in the summer. These changes allow the animal to blend into its surroundings—white against white snow, brown against brown foliage. This blending makes the animal far less vulnerable to an attack by a predator and thus more apt to survive.

Darwin's second primary pattern of survival is *individual diversity*, which simply means that with few exceptions, no two members of a species are exactly alike. The range of possible adaptations and/or innovations by individual members of a species greatly increases the species' chance of survival since more adaptive individuals are more likely to survive and procreate. In Darwin's work, the "demands of the environment" are defined as the physical requirements of a given environment, such as climate, availability of food, or protection from predators. Likewise, the term "survival" refers to the species' ability to continue to exist physically in that environment.

Certainly we, as a species, are regarded as particularly adaptive, innovative, and individually diverse, with a wide range of physical characteristics and social systems in keeping with specific environmental demands. Think of the physical and cultural differences between a nomadic tribe in the desert and the inhabitants of a South Pacific Island.

What, you now ask, does this brief explanation of the Darwinian theory of survival have to do with you? Quite simply, what is true of survival in the physical world is also true in the psychological world. Grasp the meaning of Darwin's concept of survival and you begin to understand the meaning and power of a psychological survival system. That is the basic premise of this book.

There are three important assumptions that expand the basic theory of survival, allowing for a shift from the general nature of a species' physical survival to the unique characteristics of the psychological survival of human beings.

- The first assumption is that what is true of human beings as a species is also true of individual human beings. The need, then, of a child to "survive" his or her physical and psychological environment requires, like the species in general, conformity to the demands of that environment through adaptation and innovation.

- The second assumption is that each person is a separate and unique entity with a physiological makeup and a psychological core. This is the "you" of inherent potential, the "you" who is separate and unlike any other. This individuality is a factor in determining one's style and method of adaptation and/or innovation to one's environment. It is this very individuality that creates the complexities of the survival system, as each person exists in a unique environment containing its own set of demands and adaptive requirements.

• The third assumption expands both the meaning of "the demands of the environment" and what is required for survival. In Darwin's terms, the ability to survive was paramount and based solely on the physical demands of the environment and the ability to physically survive. But the human species' higher consciousness requires more than physical survival. This unique characteristic of our species also requires adaptation and innovation to psychological environments in order to survive psychologically.

It is important to emphasize that a healthy, responsive, and supportive environment allows for a positive process of adaptation resulting in behaviors and feelings that enhance the full potential of the individual. Such an environment does not require a survival system.

The use of the terms "survival" or "need to survive," as used in this book, implies a difficult or dysfunctional environment in childhood. That is, an environment that required an adaptation diminishing or distorting the inherent potential of the individual. A survival system so defined emerges only after the child has reached a certain stage of intellectual development. This usually occurs no earlier than five or six years of age, although pieces of it may have begun earlier. It is interesting that the original Snow White fable chose "seven years" as the age of Snow White when the Queen became enraged and envious of the child's increasing beauty. The revised story of "A Tale of Survival" suggests that Snow White's need to be ugly began at that time.

Although a child's survival system becomes the later negative and self-defeating patterns of the adult, the system's importance to that child must be recognized. The system does keep the individual's physical and/or psychological core intact. And under certain circumstances, it can be more damaging for a child to react directly to the chaos of a destructive environment than to create a survival system that adapts to that environment. As you continue to read the various case histories, you will increasingly appreciate this paradox.

Explicit/Implicit Knowing and Mirror Neurons

In "A Tale of Survival," the seven-year old Snow White "knows, *without conscious awareness*, that there is danger in that mirror." The results of research in neuroscience and infant attachment have yielded important information that offers insight into how and why the child "knows." Researchers now differentiate between explicit knowing associated with the left brain and implicit knowing associated with the right brain.

Explicit knowledge is that which an individual can consciously recall and articulate; knowledge that is conscious, symbolic, declarative, and capable of being narrated; knowledge that is already known and codified. It is rooted in language and begins when language begins—around eighteen months. Explicit knowledge is the knowledge found in documents, books, manuals, etc., and is the basis of the education of reading, writing, and arithmetic. Explicit knowledge is the foundation and core of our capacity to think.

That which is *unconscious* had been conscious at one time but is now repressed. However, having once been conscious, it still falls into the domain of explicit knowledge.

Implicit knowledge is non-symbolic, non-verbal, and non-conscious, involving parts of the brain that do not require conscious processing during encoding or retrieval. In general, implicit knowing involves circuits in the brain that are tied to experiences involving behaviors, emotions, and images. Unlike explicit knowledge, implicit knowledge or knowing is present at birth.

Daniel Stern and a group known as the Boston Change Process Study Group, well-known researchers in infant attachment issues, further define implicit knowing as "relational knowing"—knowing how to be with other people. Stern explains it in this way in *The Present Moment in Psychotherapy and Everyday Life*: "Babies do not communicate in the verbal explicit register until well after eighteen months or so when they begin to talk. Accordingly, all the rich analogically nuanced, social and affective interactions that take place in the first year and a half of life occur, by default, in the implicit, non-verbal domain. Also, all the considerable knowledge that infants acquire about what to expect from people, how to deal with them, how to feel about them, and how to be with them falls into this non-verbal domain."

This ability to implicitly anticipate and respond to the other(s) creates states of mind in an infant that are encoded as an implicit form of memory. Watching an infant respond one way with mother and very differently to father is watching the effects of implicit memory. The infant has "learned" implicitly how to be with each parent based on previous interactions now embedded as implicit memory. We continue to implicitly anticipate and respond to others throughout our lifetime, continually forming implicit memories. Our lives can become shaped by reactivations of implicit memory, which lack a sense that something is being recalled. We act, feel, and imagine without recognition of the power of past experiences to define our present reality.

Mirror neurons were discovered nearly two decades ago by researchers studying the brains of monkeys. What they discovered was that a monkey, watching another monkey perform a goal-oriented action, reacted with the same brain activity as if it were performing the action, although no actual physical movement occurred. Later research studies confirmed that the human brain has multiple mirror neuron systems that react, not only to another's physical actions, but equally as well to their intentions—the social meaning of their actions and emotions. For example, when you see someone frowning, your mirror neurons for frowning also fire up. You instantaneously experience a sensation in your mind of the feeling associated with frowning. You don't have to think about what the other person intends by frowning, you experience the meaning immediately. In other words, we have the capacity to connect to the minds of others, not through reasoning, but through a process of mirroring or simulating their minds—by feeling, not thinking.

The importance of this discovery is captured by Daniel Siegel with: "As these mirror properties were discovered in humans . . . it became clear that the *human brain creates representations of other's minds*. At a neural level, we embed in our brains not just what we physically see, but the mental intention we imagine is going on in someone else's mind" (*The Mindful Brain: Reflections and Attunement in the Cultivation of Well-Being*).

Mirror neurons are seen as an important component of tribal socialization, which in turn, is vital for higher species survival. They are major factors in such emotions and activities as empathy, imitation, emulation, and language acquisition. The role mirror neurons play in a species' ability to survive by having a capacity to understand the actions, intentions, and emotions of others is also a primary survival factor in an individual child's adaptations to the actions, intentions, and emotions of others in his or her world.

The Power of Attachment

For children, there are two primary forces behind the need to adapt to the demands of their environment: *the power of attachment* and *the fear of abandonment*. Attachment refers to the relationship that forms between infants and their parents or parent substitutes. It is the bond that, at the most basic evolutionary level, allows the child to survive by seeking proximity to those who offer safety and comfort. It is the bond that allows the child to survive, physically and psychologically, for no young child can exist in isolation and without adult involvement. The attachment bond also offers the child the possibility of experiencing a positive sense of self and worth. Any threat to the continuation of the attachment bond, even momentarily, activates a strong reaction in the child. To catch the look of the fear of abandonment, watch a child's face reflect inner panic when a parent threatens to leave without the child. Or, imagine you are exploring a strange and uncharted island—and you watch the ship that brought you there sail away without you.

A child who develops a survival system in order to maintain a crucial bond of attachment will continually adjust and adapt, in subtle and unrecognizable ways, to maintain that bond. Thus, the difficult demands of a childhood environment and the original reasons for adaptation are deeply buried in the behaviors and attitudes of the individual and not easily recognized.

Let's use the "survival" Snow White as an example. If she were in therapy, the death of her mother and the absence of her father would be major areas of therapeutic concern. Since such losses can be, and usually are, traumatic for a child, therapy conceivably could offer some healing. But the powerful negative role of the stepmother, who had become Snow White's primary childhood attachment figure, would be hidden. Snow White's survival system of "needing to be ugly" would have effectively muted the reason (stepmother's need to be the fairest of all) for the child's original adaptation, with the Queen emerging from Snow White's memory as a positive and caring influence. There would be no obvious reason for Snow White's resistance to change and seemingly no way to get to the core of her problem. Asking about a hidden "need to" can begin the process of discovery.

"Whose Need Got Met?"

Donald W. Winnicott, a British pediatrician and analyst, developed a theoretical model of development that emphasized the power of attachment and the importance of the mother/infant dynamic. Of particular significance to the Survival System approach is his notion of *the good-enough mother*, a mother who is able to establish an environment in which her infant can thrive. By "good-enough" Winnicott meant that the mother provides satisfaction in response to the infant's signals. If however, the mother has not been "good-enough" and substitutes her own gesture or need for that of her infant, the infant's sense of self is distorted.

I use the "good-enough mother" concept to highlight a predominant reason for a child needing to develop a survival system. The picture of a baby, lying quite content, with the mother nearby, personifies this concept of mothering. Baby starts to feel the pangs of hunger, baby cries (signals), mother hears and understands the signal, and offers her breast. In this process, baby is allowed to experience his or her own need, signal, and have the need met. There are other kinds of mothers, including those who ignore the signals, don't understand the signals, or are too busy to respond in a reasonable time. The mother who is particularly difficult to identify as the problem is the one who wants to be *the good mother*. In this picture, baby is content, mother looks at her watch and thinks, "It's been two hours since baby ate—he must be hungry." Wanting to be a good mother, she offers her breast. Offer a breast to a baby, baby sucks. Whose need got met?

The survival system approach expands the question of "Whose need got met?" well beyond the mother/infant dynamic. It asks the question in the context of a child's development through the critical years between early childhood and adolescence. It includes the influence of not only mothers who impose their needs on a child, but fathers, siblings, other family members, and the entire range of influences upon a child. The survival system approach also raises the question of what that child needed to do or be in order to adapt to the needs of the other. The answers can unlock the mystery of why someone is unable to change.

How Children Understand Their World

Survival systems are developed in childhood. Breaking free from one's system as an adult requires an understanding of how children think, what they feel, and the origins of their fears. Having insight into the general principles of how children experience their world allows you to connect to how, as a child, you might have reacted to various demands in your environment.

Before reading about the specifics of how children think and feel, it is valuable to imagine how a child exists in his or her world.

Imagine being three feet tall and

- looking up into the angry face and pointing finger of a towering father.

- standing really tall and being eye-to-eye with the neighbor's dog.

- walking along a street and seeing, not faces, but knees and pants.

- feeling confused about the sudden appearance of Mommy's new baby.

- being certain that there are monsters in the closet.

- getting crushed and unable to breathe in Uncle Harry's hug.

Try to put yourself into the shoes of a young child as you read the experiences of the individuals in this book.

Just as a child is unable to physically perform like an adult, so a child's thinking is tied to appropriate levels of intellectual development. And young children think concretely. They do not understand the subtleties of language, so they assume a literal meaning of words. Describe a piece of clothing as "hot" and they will be afraid to touch it. Tell a young boy to stop banging on a drum and he'll stop—but then bang on a table.

Nor do children have the capacity to grasp abstract concepts. Anyone who has heard a child respond to questions like, "What happens when it rains?" or "What makes the sky blue?" knows how creative, amusing, and concrete the answers can be. Children, when experiencing something new, will understand it by matching it to a pre-existing idea or experience. Young children think of right and wrong in terms of absolutes—of things being either always good or always bad. When judging an act, the young child does not consider the intent behind the act; only the outcome, good or bad, with the judgment based on the extent of the physical damage done. When it comes to adapting to an adverse environment, concrete thinking can limit the range of adaptive possibilities.

Children believe that their parents are all-knowing and all-powerful. This belief by the child is reinforced by parental behavior. A parent will often comment on what is, to the parent, an obvious behavior, but one not obvious to the child. For example, Tim is too busy to take time out to go to the bathroom. He stands wriggling and crossing his legs. His parent says, "Please go to the bathroom," and Tim asks in wonder, "How did you know?" Since Tim's parents know everything, including his feelings and wants, there is a potential for misunderstanding. Tim can assume that his parents' lack of responsiveness is not because they don't know, but because they don't care. This trust in the perfection of the parent reinforces the child's belief that if anything is wrong, it must be with him or her and not the parent.

Children are egocentric and cannot understand another's perspective, only their own. Egocentricity leads to believing that everybody must have similar emotions, thoughts, and experiences. It also translates into, "It's all about me!" This belief is not about vanity or self-aggrandizement but about how children believe, think, and question how they exist in their worlds. It is expressed in questions, such as: "Do they like me?" "Do I fit in?" "Do I play ball well enough?" "Am I tall enough?" "Am I pretty enough?" "Am I too serious?" "Am I not serious enough?" and so on. Their egocentricity leads them to believe that they are the center of their world and that they have imaginary powers to affect that world. Ask a young child why the sun comes up and the answer will be, "Because it is time for me to get out of bed." In keeping with that belief, they also believe they are responsible for what is happening in that world. Young children's immature concepts of cause and effect often connect to their natural egocentrism, often leading to emotionally damaging feelings of guilt as they mistakenly blame themselves for a divorce, illness, or another catastrophe. I remember working with a couple who had decided to get a divorce and sought help in how to minimize the effect of the divorce on their six-year-old boy. Both parents consistently reinforced basic points to their child—that they both loved him, that the divorce was between Mommy and Daddy, and that he wasn't responsible for their separating. One night, the baby-sitter reported that their son's friend was banging on a drum. Caught in the belief that he was responsible for his parent's problems, the boy told his friend: "Don't make so much noise. My daddy left because I was making too much noise." One young boy captured the power of this belief of responsibility when he said, "I know here (pointing to his head) I'm not to blame—but here (pointing to his heart) I know I am." Such is the thought process of the child.

Parents can unknowingly feed into this egocentricity by the way they relate to their child. An example of this is how children respond to their parents' silence. For example, imagine a couple who have realized that an important investment has lost its value—causing each to be quite upset. Neither one is ready to discuss the ramifications of the loss or what steps need to be taken—so both parents remain silent.

Playing quietly by herself is their eight-year-old daughter. The child can feel the negative energy in the room, observe her parents' upset faces, know something is wrong—thinking concretely and matching it to a pre-existing experience—and assume that her parents are angry. Experiencing the negative vibrations in keeping with her egocentric thinking, she then assumes that she must be the cause of the problem. She begins to imagine various scenarios in which she had caused a problem that in turn caused her parents to become angry in the past, and she begins to get fussy and agitated. Her parents become aware of her agitation and, speaking in authoritative voices, caution her to "go find something to do"—thus reinforcing her idea of herself as being to blame for the problem.

To illustrate how a child understands and interprets the behavior of adults, let's take a look at a six-year old we'll call Eric. Eric's father provides for his family and loves his children. However, his father is an alcoholic. His father's excessive drinking pains and embarrasses Eric, particularly when it causes family arguments. Eric cannot grasp the abstraction of addiction and therefore cannot understand why his father drinks. As a child, he naturally assumes the fault lies in something that relates to him. Eric says to himself, "If my father really loved me, he wouldn't drink." But Eric doesn't stop there, silently continuing with, "If I were a better basketball player (or a better student, or taller, or . . .) then he would love me and then he wouldn't drink." Thus Eric not only feels the pain of his father's drinking, but the pain of having caused it. A possible system he would develop could be one of always being the "good boy" in order not to disappoint anyone, or conversely, the "bad boy" in order to have a reason for his father's not loving him.

Many of the distortions that come from childhood—how children think, learn, and solve problems—are the hidden continuing distortions of adulthood. The story of Alice illustrates this point. Alice's parents each had their own history of a childhood caught in negative competition, centering on who was the one with the "true expertise." Alice's mother played it out overtly by being the expert in all matters; father, covertly, by raising some question that would effectively undermine the mother, or any expert. Alice, responding to all the negative vibrations, and thinking in the normal egocentric ways of childhood, became a very responsible child so as to not upset her parents. Fast-forward to today, and Alice is now an adult, married, with an eight-year-old child. The child has been getting into trouble in school—is seen as a "difficult child"—primarily because of her refusal to accept any responsibility for her negative behavior in the classroom and with her classmates. Alice seeks professional help in order to learn how to help her child and discovers that she is the primary source of the problem. Neither of her parents could tolerate being the individual who was responsible for any negative consequence to their "expert" standing. Alice, being the "responsible child," filled the void caused by no one's assumption of responsibility by becoming the one member of the family who immediately assumed all responsibility for anything that went wrong or wasn't right. She unknowingly carried that reaction into adulthood and had been assuming the negative responsibility of her own child. It was *her* fault that the child did this or that—if *she* were a better mother, the child would not be a problem. In other words, she continued to relate to her child the way she had related to, and gotten caught in, her parents' dysfunction. As she realized this and began to let the child assume responsibility appropriately, the child ceased being a problem.

Developing a New Approach

The survival system approach expands Darwin's theory to include both psychological and physical survival, as well as the survival needs of individual human beings in response to the demands of their childhood environments. Implicit "relational" knowing teaches the child how to be with—and survive—the other. The survival necessity of continued attachment drives a survival system. Winnicott's theory asks the key question: *Whose need got met?* And the mixture of egocentricity and concrete thinking can lead children to misinterpret their worlds in many ways. The following examples capture the significance of all of the above:

A child doesn't say, "My mother is suffering from depression."

Depression is an abstraction, and abstractions are beyond the capacity of the child's understanding. Thinking concretely, what the child feels is that "I'm not good enough to make my mother happy." The child may begin to internalize a survival system of being "good enough" by becoming an especially good child, sensitive to mother's moods, never making mistakes, not expressing needs, and attempting to do everything perfectly. In other words, the child becomes caught in a survival system of *needing to be perfect*.

A child doesn't say, "My father is addicted to making a fortune." Addiction is an abstraction. What the child believes is, "I don't count for very much in my father's life." The internal drive then would be to prove his or her worth. A possible survival system would be *a need to succeed*, at the cost of personal growth.

A child doesn't say, "My mother is a controlling person—or my mother needs to have me need her." Children don't think of parents as having dysfunctional needs. What the child believes is, "Mother makes all of the decisions because she loves me and doesn't want me to make a mistake." Underneath that belief is the hidden implicit message from the mother that "If you want me to love you (attachment bond), you must need me." Possible survival system: *a need to be dependent*.

A child doesn't say, "My father is competitive and always has to win." What the child feels is, "I can't do anything right, no matter how hard I try." Responding to his own sense of failure, as well as the implicit competitive vibrations from the father, the child avoids challenges, commitments, and personal growth. Possible survival system: *a need to not take anything seriously*.

A child's sense of survival is dependent upon the stability of the adults in his world. From the child's point of view, it is more comforting to believe that he is the problem rather than to recognize the instability or irrationality of his parents. A child's egocentricity allows him then to hold on to some sense of hope, for if he is responsible, then he can also make it right. "Maybe this time, if I don't make noise, Mom and Dad won't fight and scream at each other." And silently, without being aware of it, he finishes the thought with, "And then I will be safe."

This is the essence of a survival system: the psychological and/or physical adaptation of the child to the difficult or dysfunctional world around him, driven by an implicit knowing of how to be with the other, as well as a powerful need for continued attachment, understood on the basis of concrete thinking and interpreted through the egocentric vision appropriate to a seven-year-old.

In reading this book and in analyzing your own survival system, you must keep in mind the process of how a child implicitly knows, thinks, and feels. Keep in mind as well that what has been acting as a barrier to your full potential as an adult may well have been the adaptation that "saved" you as a child.

CHAPTER FOUR

Beginning to Change the Opponent

POINTS TO MAKE
ACTIONS TO TAKE

C ase histories offer valuable insight into how and why various individuals had needed to not be, get, or achieve what they wanted. The cases also trace the necessary steps taken by these individuals to uncover and dismantle their survival systems. In this and other chapters like it, the primary dynamics of a case—points to make—are emphasized and expanded to offer suggestions—actions to take—for your beginning to understand, confront, and change your survival system.

Survival systems are complex, inner structures representing the subtle differences between individuals, their environments, and the quality of their interactions. This complexity explains why the same environmental demand can be met by several different adaptive systems; and the same behavior pattern may be meeting different environmental demands. To help you understand this important concept, I have included several vignettes of the struggles of other patients in the chapters dealing with change. These mini-case histories augment the information found in the major case histories and illustrate how creative children can be in developing survival systems. In recognizing the systems of all of the individuals mentioned, as well as the ways they used various techniques and tools to break free, you will be able to gain the necessary insight and information to free yourself and change what has been unchangeable.

Point: When you ask the question: "Do I need, for some unknown reason, to . . . ?" the answer can act as a guide in discovering your survival system. The phrase, "for some unknown reason," would refer to the hidden environmental demand of your childhood. The blank space would represent the behavior that was the innovation/adaptation that you, as a child, developed to meet that demand. The clues in solving the mystery of why people stop themselves from getting what they want are to be found in the persistent, self-defeating behaviors of those individuals. This is particularly true when these negative behavior patterns are in sharp contrast to what the person repeatedly says he or she wants. In the language of the detective novel, it would read—follow the behavior.

In Beth's case, the "environmental demand" was her father's dysfunctional need for Beth to assume the role of surrogate wife and mother of the family. As such, she was not available for a marriage of her own. Her adaptation/innovation was to remain "ugly," with her feelings about her weight and looks effectively keeping her from socializing and being open to meeting eligible men. She maintained the power of her system by defeating any changes she attempted. In following Beth's behavior, it was clear that she was not free to have a life of her own.

Beth's system was particularly resistant to change because her need to not be married was being actively reinforced by her father in her adult life. Hers is a good example of the enormous power of a survival system and its continuing hold over the individual. Her dramatic breakthrough began because of a powerful shift in her belief system. As a child she had implicitly believed that, in order to survive, she must become and remain what her father needed her to be. The power of that belief was negated when she experienced the "sign" that God, who had more power than the internalized father of her childhood, wanted her to live.

In Beth's case, the power came from her religious beliefs; but any form of empowerment which redirects you can be the seed that starts the process of breaking free. The steps Beth took were directed toward establishing her own identity through finding a new job, leaving the community, moving into her own apartment, resisting the pressures of her siblings and parents, and successfully improving her appearance. These steps led to a healthy separation from her family and an increased availability to appropriate, eligible men.

Action: Start to "follow the behavior" that consistently defeats your attempts to change and start asking the key question: "Do I need, for some unknown reason, to not get what I want?" Begin to analyze your behavior patterns as they relate to achieving your wants and goals and look for specific behaviors that are particularly effective in maintaining the status quo. Pay attention and try to bring to your conscious awareness, ideas, attitudes, and beliefs that are also involved in meeting an archaic environmental demand of your childhood. Shift your thinking from *you* being the problem to *an unknown factor* of your past being the problem.

Another way of approaching the who and what, of the problem is to put the question into a situation where a physical condition is causing you to not be able to achieve a desired goal. You would analyze the symptoms you were having (the

behaviors and beliefs), see them as clues and indicators of the
actual physical problem (the survival system), and begin to take
steps to heal the condition (achieve your potential).

Point: Your changing can challenge the existing dynamics
between you and the others in your world and result in their
having a strong negative reaction to the "new you." Beth's
father was so furious at her establishing her own family that
he caused a permanent break in their relationship. As you read
through the various stories, you will find other examples of
how family members reacted to a changing system.

Action: Ask yourself if there are negative consequences to
breaking free from your survival system. One way of teasing
out the answers is to pose the question: "If I had a magic wand
and could make my wants a reality, what would change? Would
there be any danger to myself, or to someone else, if the magic
worked?"

The immediate answer usually is: "Of course there's no
danger in getting what I want." But a survival system is in
response to the demands of someone or something else. The
"wants" of an individual caught in a system are not achievable
as long as power rests, or is perceived to rest, in the other
"someone" or "something." Asking about the possibility of
getting your "wants" can point to who or what might have
been, or still is, the "other."

Imagining the possible results of change can reveal hidden
dangers. Beth's getting what she wanted caused repercussions
in her parents' marriage and created a permanent rift between
herself and her father. As an adult, Beth was able to tolerate
his reaction. As a child, she would have felt the extreme fear of
abandonment.

Point: Defining the nature and power of the other's need
is a crucial step in understanding your need for not getting
yours met. Some need of a parent or other family member can

be particularly powerful and account for the corresponding power of the resulting survival system. For example, Beth got caught in her father's need for her to remain "a shadow wife—a shadow mother." His presence in her adult life allowed him to continue to exert his power, reinforced by his "generosity." The survival system of Snow White was in response to the narcissism of her stepmother.

Narcissism is a particularly powerful force that is almost guaranteed to create a corresponding reaction in children. Let's take a moment to look at narcissism in the context of a survival system. In the Greek myth, a beautiful young boy named Narcissus is unable to love or relate to another, even though others fall in love with him. One day he sees his reflection in a pool of water and, unaware that he is looking at himself, becomes enamored of the beautiful face he sees. The world and all within it fall away as he becomes obsessed with the image he has seen. Ultimately he dies of longing, turning into the flower we call narcissus.

Narcissistic individuals are driven by their need to be desired and admired. Characteristics that are usually associated with narcissism include: a grandiose sense of self-importance; an expectation of and demand for special treatment; a belief that one's problems are unique; dreams of unlimited success, power, beauty, or ideal love; a lack of empathy; and feelings of envy. Fearing any loss of their specialness, narcissists are easily injured and outraged when they feel they are not understood or valued. Thus, the narcissism of a parent, stepparent, grandparent, sibling, or other significant family member traps the child in the other's obsession of self. The message the narcissist sends is that he or she is the center of, and the most important object in, the universe. The role of anyone else must be secondary and non-competitive. Such messages lead to childhood survival systems of needing to minimize potential in order to avoid the other's withdrawal or rage.

Action: Begin a new understanding of your childhood by remembering and observing the people with whom you shared that environment. Certainly anyone who fits a narcissistic profile would have been a key player in your survival system. It can be helpful to imagine that you are a character in a movie: How does the plot play? Do the characters seem authentic? Who plays the roles of hero, heroine, or villain? Is the movie a mystery, comedy, tragedy, or war-picture? In what "role" have you been cast? Looking at your life this way gives you more objectivity and a better look at your hidden need for a survival system.

Point: The hallmark of a survival system is your persistent need to be stuck. One image of stuckness is of someone caught at the bottom of a deep hole, dug in sand. The more the person tries to climb up the wall of sand, the more the sand shifts. The manifestation of a survival system is the *"yes/but"* syndrome. The stuck person says "yes" to positive suggestions, while countering with a "but," followed by a reason for non-action. As an example, here is how a conversation with Beth would sound:

Beth: "It's time for me to get my body in shape."

Friend: "What about joining a gym?"

Beth: "*Yes*, that's a good idea, *but* I can't afford it right now."

Friend: "There are lots of specials being offered."

Beth: "*Yes*, I saw one in the paper this morning. *But*, it's probably not legitimate. Maybe (*yes*) I could pick up some extra money working overtime. *But* then I wouldn't have time to go to the gym."

She remains stuck.

Action: Learn how to counter the "yes/but" syndrome by using it against itself. In the example above, Beth counters every positive suggestion with a negative "but." To break the syndrome, she needs to say "yes" to the negative, followed by a positive suggestion. For example:

> Beth: "*But*, it's probably not legitimate. (*Yes*) A lot of those offers are phony, *but* maybe I can find one that is honest."

> Beth: "*But* then I wouldn't have time to go to the gym. (*Yes*) I guess that could be a problem, *but* maybe I can go during my lunch hour."

Each time you manage a shift in your thinking, your survival system will be slightly undermined. Become conscious of how often you say, aloud or to yourself, "yes/but." Find a way to articulate the problem in a positive way, countering the negative with a positive. Also listen for the yes/buts in the reactions of the people around you, particularly if you are trying to change.

Point: There can be other behavior patterns that meet the same environmental demand. Beth's environmental demand was that she not be married and have a family of her own. Another patient of mine, Frank, had a system of unavailability that was as effective in meeting that demand as Beth's system of needing to be ugly.

Frank, in his early forties, had long wanted to settle down and start raising a family. But his profession kept him traveling, with his constant trips affecting his relationships with women. The few serious relationships he had over the years ended in friendships, not marriage, and he had begun to believe that he was stuck in permanent bachelorhood. That is, until his survival system was exposed when he began to remember what had seemed an insignificant moment from years ago. He recalled that when he was nine years old, his father and mother had divorced. On the day his father moved out of the family home, he took Frank aside and said, "Frank, I'm leaving to take a new job up North. Mom and the girls are now your responsibility." Frank, as a child, took his father's words literally and had been carrying that responsibility ever since. Like Beth, he could not have a marriage and family of his own since he was a "father and husband" already. His adaptation/innovation was to be constantly on the move and therefore unavailable for a lasting relationship.

Another environmental demand that feeds a system of unavailability is one that sends a secret parental message requiring that you remain available to them. A particular child, often a girl, is secretly designated the future "caretaker" of the parents in their later years. The child, now grown, develops a career, travels, and seems to have a full life. However, she remains single and never moves out of the parental home, appearing to be uninterested in establishing a home of her own.

Action: Recognize the effects of how children think. As a child, Frank's (mis)understanding of what his father had said serves as a powerful example. Remember, children understand language concretely and do not have the capacity to distinguish between the actual words and the abstract meaning behind the words. Start to question how you may have (mis)interpreted the meaning of some of your childhood experiences. Question also if being unable to meet your adult needs is tied to secret messages of earlier parental needs.

Point: Do not underestimate the power of a survival system. A survival adaptation that began in childhood has an incredible hold on an individual for the very fact that it is rooted in beliefs of survival. Those beliefs do not change easily for they are deeply imbedded in the psyche and behavior of an individual.

Action: Be patient with the process and with yourself. Remember that uncovering a survival system will take time and a good deal of creative investigation. You have much to gain—rediscovering your potential.

How do you start?

PART TWO

The Three Basic Elements of a Survival System

INDIVIDUALITY

THE ENVIRONMENT OF YOUR CHILDHOOD

THE INTERACTION

CHAPTER FIVE

His Individuality

W hat a handsome man, I thought, as I greeted Mark for the first time. He grinned a winning smile as he walked into my office. I knew from our initial phone conversation that he was an actor, and he had the look of a successful one. This early impression was reinforced for the first several sessions as Mark related his history.

The Need to Be "Second-Banana:" Mark

He was the second son of successful parents, his father an architect, his mother a business executive. Considered bright and academically advanced, he was placed in the gifted student program throughout his school years. In high school he had been involved in a number of extra-curricular activities including the school's theater program for which he had written and starred in a number of play productions. In recognition of his popularity and accomplishments, Mark had been voted as the student most likely to succeed by his graduating class. Besides being bright, Mark was clearly multi-talented. He was an accomplished actor, dancer, and singer. When only twenty-two years of age, and fresh out of college, he had secured a part in a successful Broadway musical. For the next several years he alternated between performing on the stage and in television. He also seemed to have an extensive network of successful friends in the entertainment industry.

So I was surprised when, in answer to a question about his current living arrangements, he answered, "I'm living with my folks." His potential for success seemed to have been buried in a series of subsequent failed roles, lost opportunities, and poor choices. Despite his attempts to be self-sufficient and his brief flirtation with success, he was still financially dependent on his parents. So much for early impressions!

But how odd that someone with so much potential and an early career boost would be forced to live, at age twenty-six, with his parents. As Mark talked about his professional struggles, a theme did begin to emerge—a theme of consistently choosing the wrong path. In the beginning, Mark went after roles as singer/dancer/actor in musicals and variety shows and succeeded in establishing the beginnings of a solid reputation. But somewhere along the way he shifted his focus, dropped his musical interests, and began to audition for more serious acting roles. Over a two-year period, he went from a known performer to a non-working actor and eventually was dropped by his agent. At the start of our meetings, Mark wasn't sure how to jump-start his career.

Listening to him talk about his career, my impression was that he lacked the passion necessary for becoming a successful dramatic actor and that his true interest lay in musical dramas, not only as performer, but as composer and lyricist as well. I began to wonder if he was caught in a survival system. Was he unconsciously sabotaging his promising career? I told him the two tales of Snow White and began to listen for "vibrations of envy" in his childhood environment. But as Mark shared his history with me, it became clear that envy was not a factor—quite the opposite. His family was genuinely proud of his accomplishments and no one seemed to be sending a message that would require his minimizing his talent. If anything, the reverse was true, for there was an expectation that he would be famous one day.

One message that did come across was the concern Mark felt for his mother and his sympathy for the pressures under which she had labored when he was growing up. She had worked steadily from the time of her marriage, at first putting her husband through graduate school. By the time he had established his practice, she had reached a top executive position and had decided to continue in her career. Mark's father devoted most of his time and energy to his work and, when home, was unavailable to the family. His brother, fourteen months his senior, had a history of chronic asthma and appears to have had a childhood affinity for breaking his bones. Mark's maternal grandmother had "life-threatening" illnesses for as long as he could remember, with his mother called upon to take care of each crisis. (Grandma kept going strong until ninety-five.)

Could he have squashed his own career to be available to act as a support for his mother? We pursued that possibility but soon recognized that wasn't the case. As far as we could tell, Mark's mother had not relied on him, and he had not been especially available to her. There was, however, a "something" in his connection with his mother that continued to elude us. What I had begun to recognize was how acutely aware Mark was of me, and my reactions to him. It was an awareness that went beyond normal patient interest and curiosity. Because Mark worked in the theater, I found it useful to use terminology and images from that profession. And because of my own earlier work in the theater, I had learned how to be conscious of the subtleties found in interactions—what performers call "the space between." The reality of a scene is not created by an individual actor but in the space between two actors. It is this interactive space to which the audience responds. I shared my "space between" imagery with Mark, as well as my sense of his awareness of me. I asked him what reality he thought was being played out between us—what reality he might be putting in that space?

"I imagine," he said, "that you've got all kinds of ideas about me."

"Why would you think that?"

"Because most people jump to conclusions. For example, you're probably thinking that there must be something wrong with me. That my primary problem is that I've been too enmeshed in my family—too concerned about my mother."

"Do you usually assume to know what I'm thinking and give my thoughts a judgmental twist?"

"I do it a lot," he confessed.

I told him that he was wrong about what I was thinking, that I didn't think that his family was the primary problem, and wasn't sure what was keeping him from reaching his potential. But I encouraged him to share his assumptions with me and that I, in turn, would be absolutely honest in sharing my reactions.

And so we developed a new way of relating. We would start to talk about a subject—he would interject his assumptions as to my reaction—I would share what I was feeling or thinking, usually quite different from his projection—and then we would continue. Slowly our "space-between" became safer for him, and we began to uncover the first layer of his reason to minimize his potential.

At some point I realized that I had a considerable amount of information about his childhood and family history but little of his world outside the family. On the surface he appeared to have an active social life, with close male and female friends. But he had no history of any significant relationships.

I asked Mark whether he was interested in establishing a long-term relationship. He was quiet for a while. "I had a girlfriend in high school but that's about it." He paused, "I'm not particularly interested in meeting anyone. I kind of like to be free and footloose."

My continued questions about his social life elicited increasingly vague and evasive answers. It seemed to me that we were dancing around the subject of his sexuality when Mark said, "I wonder if you think I'm gay."

I told him that the thought had crossed my mind.

"Would it be a problem for you?" he asked.

"Why would it be a problem?"

"Because you might be uncomfortable in this territory," he answered.

I felt that I was being given a bias that didn't belong to me. As promised, I shared my reaction. "We both know that the theater is one of the few places that tends to be fairly free of homophobia. I lived in that world for too long not to have worked out most of my biases. I have a feeling that *you're* the homophobic one, not me." His immediate reaction was one of embarrassment, but then he laughed, genuinely pleased with my response.

"I never thought of myself in those terms," he said, "but maybe you're right."

And from this exchange came a slow exploration of his sexuality.

"I remember," he said one day, "that we used to live in a pretty rough neighborhood. I was about seven or eight. And the tough boys, the ones who went around strutting, would tease me and call me a sissy and a faggot. I wasn't sure what that word meant, but I knew it wasn't a compliment. It was around that time, or maybe even a little earlier, that I began to feel that somehow I was different."

Mark began to reveal how he had experienced himself as being different. He wasn't interested in what his brother and other boys seemed to like—things like baseball, football, wrestling, and fighting. He enjoyed playing with girls and would sometimes imagine what it was like to be a girl.

I asked him if he had become interested in boys when he reached adolescence.

"Not really," he replied. "I don't think I've ever been interested in or sexually involved with either sex."

It seemed to me that Mark was caught in a quandary. He wasn't sexually interested in females because he was gay and, on some conscious level, knew it. But for some unknown reason, he was unable to allow himself to act on this knowledge.

There seemed to be a discrepancy as well, between Mark's inability to fully acknowledge his homosexuality, his homophobic attitude, and the world in which he now existed. True, his experience of being put down by the neighborhood bullies was painful; but his current world was generally free of prejudice, and his family did not appear to share his views. Why the powerfully negative ideas of homosexuality? It was a question to which Mark had no answer.

We found a clue to his survival system in a seemingly innocent story about Mark's experiences in elementary school. One of his teachers had commented in class that, "It was a shame that such thick, curly, black eyelashes were wasted on a boy."

He seemed overly sensitive to that comment, even now as he related it, some twenty years later. I asked him why it bothered him so much.

"Because," he answered, "she's implying that I got more than my share."

"Your share of what?"

"Everything," he said.

Our session ended, but his words continued to echo in my mind. What did he mean by that last exchange? I vaguely remembered an article I had once read about an accomplished actor, musician, playwright—referred to by the writer as a true "renaissance man"—and the pain this individual expressed at having experienced the reaction of others to his having more than his due.

I shared my thoughts with Mark at our next session. I asked him if it was possible that the "unknown environmental demand" for his system was to be found in his belief that he had been given too much.

As is so often the case, Mark's initial reaction was one of skepticism. "I'm not sure that really applies to me," he said. And he put the idea to one side as he pursued other more current issues with which he was struggling. But my question had touched a nerve, for in a later session he began to talk about how difficult it must have been for his brother to have a brother like him.

"I felt sorry for my brother," he said. "He was supposed to be the older brother and he sometimes played that role. He'd tackle me, hold me down, and remind me that he was the big brother. But the truth was that I developed early, and by the time he went off to school, I was taller and more physically developed than he. Then he had this asthmatic condition that limited a lot of his activities, and I was an especially healthy kid. And to top it all off, I skipped some of the early grades, landing up in the same class year as he."

"In other words," I said, "you got more than your share."

"I guess so," he replied, "when you put it that way. I imagine I could have felt that I had been given too much."

It was during our explorations of his getting too much that we started to use "second-banana" as a code word for what appeared to be a survival system of needing to be less. By definition, second-bananas play a subordinate role to the lead character, and Mark seemed to have expanded this notion to his entire life. Each subsequent session offered some example of how he felt he had been given too much—good looks, intelligence, good grades, talent, a winning personality, an ability to make friends, and so on. And each example offered another way he had played second-banana to someone else, particularly in his career. But getting too much didn't fully explain the power of his system or his prejudice about homosexual men.

Mark and I went round and round about this last point, both missing an essential connection to his system—until several movies and plays were produced, having homosexual themes, with actors openly playing gay men. In a casual conversation that touched on our mutual interest in the theater, I mentioned one of these plays. Mark's immediate reaction was negative, not to the play itself, but to the way the actors played the gay characters.

I asked him if he was bothered by the way the actors acted or the characters the actors were portraying.

"It's all the same," he said. "It's all about their being too damn much."

There it was, the essential connection. He hadn't said the characters had been overwritten, or the actors overacted. He blended character, performer, and performance and said—*they were too much*. Like piecing together a difficult picture puzzle, we began to make sense of the jumble of clues we had been struggling to understand.

Clue: His need to be asexual. We found the answer in his beliefs as to what it meant to be gay and who the models were upon whom he was basing his impressions. They turned out to be gay men seen as flamboyant and wild, reinforcing a negative stereotype of a group who were "too much."

Clue: The "something" in the connection to his mother. Mark's empathy for and sensitivity to what he perceived as his mother's burdens, required that *he* not be a burden. He saw his father's unavailability and volatility, his brother's asthma and broken bones, his grandmother's frequent life-threatening illnesses, as well as the pressures of his mother's job, as all being too much for her. Since he experienced himself as already having too much, he needed to function in a way that would not make his mother feel that he, too, was too much. This belief generalized into his being unable to meet his needs and wants if he felt that they would become a problem or burden for another. Given this belief, it was not difficult to imagine how, in as competitive a field as the entertainment industry, Mark would have had to dim his talents.

Clue: His sensitivity to the plight of his older brother. Mark realized that he could have turned the tables on his brother, pinning the older boy down and proclaiming himself to be the more powerful one. But he didn't want to humiliate his brother and chose to play the weaker, younger sibling—the second banana.

Clue: The conflict between his family's expectations of him and his belief that if he lived his full potential, he would be too much for them.

Clue: His financial dependency on his parents was both a reason for, and a result of, his system. Keeping his abilities to a minimum resulted in his not getting acting or other well-paying positions. And how could he be seen as being too much if he was unable to exist on his own?

The picture that emerged was of a young, sensitive, and empathetic boy who had been acutely aware of the differences between his resources and that of others, particularly his older brother. Distorting his understanding of his considerable potential, his sense of being different, and his fear of being judged as having more than he was entitled to, he believed that not only had he been born with too much, he was in danger of turning into someone who *was* too much—a someone who took up too much space and time and who would eventually look like one of the blown-up characters in Macy's Thanksgiving Day Parade. Mark, fearing that he was too much, needed to be far less than he was.

Mark had begun to make small changes in his life before we began to understand the meaning of the "too much" material. He was able to find a job indirectly involved in entertainment, had bought himself a car, and had started looking for his own apartment. Concurrent with the months of our uncovering the true reasons for his system, Mark had returned to the challenges of his high school days and rediscovered his interest in musical drama. He created a one-man show for himself, featuring original songs and material he had written.

The reviews the day after opening night confirmed what we both had sensed—Mark was on his way to becoming a top-banana.

CHAPTER SIX

Understanding Individuality

The individuality variables that account for a defined set of physical and psychological characteristics, talents, abilities, and potentials of an individual form the first element of a survival system. Think of it this way:

We are all born with two eyes, two eyebrows, one nose, one mouth, and one chin. Yet each of us has a look that is uniquely our own. We may have features that are similar to those of someone else, but there is an identifiable look to the way our face is arranged. We are recognized as having a specific identity, of having a name that goes with the face. Just as there is an identifiable look to the way each face is arranged, so is there a psychological identity based on our personality and emotional nature. The face and body that look back from the mirror is the *physical "me."* My sense of "who" resides in that face and body is the *psychological "me."* Unlike the physical "me" which exists in space and can be seen, the psychological "me" can only be experienced.

Capturing the essence of this experience has challenged many philosophers and theorists. Expressions such as "the soul"—"the self"—"the essential being"—and others, have all been used to capture the psychological "me."

If our childhood had offered a healthy environment in which to grow, the full potential of our physical and psychological self would have been free to develop. But if the environment had presented some kind of perceived danger requiring an adaptation, the fully developed "me" might have needed to stay hidden on the dark side of the moon. What would then be presented to the world would not be our true self. If the wicked Queen had asked, "Mirror, mirror, on the wall, who is *smartest* of us all?" Snow White's survival system would have demanded that she be *stupid*.

Although there is no general agreement among researchers as to which specific factors constitute "individuality," they all agree that the uniqueness of the individual is due to characteristics that can be classified under the general categories of:

▸ *physical makeup*, such as height, weight, body build, facial features, color, and texture of hair and skin;

▸ *personality traits*, such as shy, impetuous, inquisitive, kind, generous, moody, imaginative;

▸ *emotional nature*, which includes levels of sensitivity and reactivity, the latter meaning how an individual responds to new people and unfamiliar situations.

These characteristics range along a continuum from "very high" to "very low," allowing then for a particular child to be seen as very tall, somewhat tall, somewhat short, very short, or very shy, somewhat shy, somewhat sociable, very sociable, and so on. The configuration of a multitude of physical and psychological characteristics accounts for much of our sense of a physical and psychological "me."

Physical Makeup

Of the characteristics that comprise the uniqueness of a child, physical makeup shows the most obvious individual variations and is the most rooted in the biology of the child. The role that physical variables play in the development of a Survival System is in their acceptance or rejection by others. Each culture, group, or family has its own value system relating to physical appearance. It is this value system that plays a part in how someone experiences his or her worth, and what he or she needs to do in order to survive. For example, our current culture places enormous emphasis on the value of female thinness. This value is repeatedly reinforced through advertising, movies, and television. To be desirable is to be thin. To be successful is to be thin. To be popular is to be thin. It is difficult then, if not impossible, for some non-slender girls, some as young as seven or eight, not to feel negative about their body image and therefore about themselves. This would be like taking a direct hit with the consequences leading many to develop eating disorders in an attempt to remain unnaturally thin. But an adaptation (ducking) to the pressure to be thin might take the form of a child shutting off feelings in order to minimize self-hate. That reaction is not unlike shutting off a water or gas valve when there is danger. The reaction then to a negative "fit" of being physically rounded in a thin, flat world of fashion might lead to a system of "needing not to feel or care."

In the example just given, the value of thinness is an acknowledged environmental pressure. There can also be less obvious pressures to conform to a standard in a group and/ or family. Take the issue of body hair for a young man. The age at which he needs to begin to shave, the thickness of his beard, and the amount of hair on his chest—signs of physical maturation—can become distorted determinants in judging his level of masculinity. When masculinity is equated to such a physical characteristic, a late bloomer in a family of early-maturing boys, or a young man not genetically destined to have much body hair is vulnerable to experiencing himself as less masculine than his father, brothers, or other male family members. A survival system might take the form of "needing to be tough."

Another example of needing a survival response to a less obvious pressure to conform is the child born with several features that are the opposite of the "look" of the family and group. Sally, born with blond hair, green eyes, and a pre-set for a tall, thin body was born into a family and group where dark hair, dark eyes, and a pre-set for shorter, heavier bodies was the norm. Sally was seen as somewhat of an "alien" and never felt a sense of acceptance and belonging—either by her family or cultural group. A survival system could take the form of "needing to be needed." A child of a particular ethnic or racial group, who has been adopted and loved by a couple associated with a group holding strong prejudicial biases, could feel a similar sense of being an outsider when the group expresses those biases in the presence of the child. A survival system might take the form of "needing to be deaf" outside of the home.

What these examples signify is the possibility of a need for adaptation when individuals experience a negative congruence between their innate physical attributes and the demands of their environments. This is particularly true during the adolescent years. Such examples include: being a very short boy in a world of tall heroes; being a very tall girl in a world of petite heroines; having large breasts in a world of flat-chested females; and, conversely, being flat-chested in a world of large breasts. Self-consciousness about one's physical "me" is rooted in experiencing that "me" as being not only different, but "less than."

Personality Traits and Emotional Nature

The following overview will help you understand the roles personality and emotionality play in the development of "custom-made" adaptive systems.

We start with *temperament*, which is seen as a biological potential for behavior, expressed by the predominant moods of individuals and the intensity of their activities. The concept of temperament is generally used in research with infants and very young children and relates to individual differences in characteristic patterns of infant behavior and responsiveness, particularly in the areas of infant sociability, levels of activity, positive and negative emotionality, positive and negative reactivity, and adaptability to the familiar/ unfamiliar. A temperament trait does not necessarily derive from only one genetic characteristic but is often the result of a complex interplay of multiple factors. For example, an infant isn't born exhibiting an innate temperament of positive emotionality. Instead, the temperament trait evolves from a core tendency toward positive emotionality reinforced by more subtle physiological tendencies, such as sensitivity to touch and sound, physical agility, muscle tone, and degree of alertness.

Researchers agree that the early development of temperament is the result of subtle interactions between the biology of infants and their caregivers. It is not nature versus nurture but nature *and* nurture interacting in reciprocal ways to evolve into specific patterns of existence. The manner in which an infant processes a sensation and/or an experience, and responds accordingly, will influence the adult's reactions to the infant, which in turn initiates a new series of responses in the infant. In other words, infants are not just passive receivers, but play an active part in the development and enfolding of their own temperaments. As we shall soon see, this pattern of reciprocity remains active throughout a child's development.

As the child reaches a higher level of maturity, researchers begin to use "personality" or "personality traits" to refer to inherent characteristics. These words refer to a complex pattern of psychological characteristics and behaviors expressed across time and in many different situations. They encompass a broader range of behaviors and emotions that take into account the child's initial temperament and the process of maturation. As children develop more sophisticated motor and cognitive skills, expand their use of language and increase their capabilities, they develop and express new personality traits. For example, a trait such as aggression is not possible without the motor and language skills that allow the child to direct aggressive actions toward others. The trait of dominance does not develop until a child begins to interact with other children.

The evolution of an individual's original temperament into a later more differentiated personality is a dynamic process, with each stage of a child's development offering new possibilities for the emergence of new traits. As with the emergence of infant temperament, personality is also affected and modified by an individual's interactions with his or her environment. Thus, a child with a predisposition for shyness will have that trait reinforced and intensified if the parents overprotect the child. Conversely, that same child interacting with parents who encourage, even gently push, the child toward social situations will become far less socially inhibited. Personality is also modified by someone in the environment reacting to the individual. For example, parents, teachers, and peers often respond differently to a highly sociable child versus a child who is very aggressive. The other's response, in turn, may evoke a stronger positive or negative reaction in the child, thus reinforcing a particular personality trait.

The results of temperament/personality research confirm that an individual's predisposition toward an emotional state such as fear, or a behavior such as aggression, has a genetic and biological basis involving complex physiological, neurological, biochemical, and hormonal components. This conclusion offers greater insight into the development of the psychological "me" and how that "me" would interact with the world.

The following discussion is a synthesis of several theoretical models and presents various dimensions of personality and emotional tendencies, along with their expression in behaviors and moods that most researchers have defined as being consistent characteristics of an individual. It is organized as follows:

1. There are five broad, higher-order dimensions of personality that encompass a wide range of behaviors and moods.

    These include:

    *   positive emotionality
    *   negative emotionality
    *   constraint
    *   activity level
    *   agreeableness/openness to experience

2. The higher-order dimension may encompass one or more subcategories of so-called lower-order traits and are described by their associated behaviors.

3. Each dimension and category has a range of behaviors from high (positive) to low (negative).

For example, the broad category of *positive emotionality* refers to the capacity of children to be actively and positively involved with the world around them. Within this broad category are several sub-categories, one of which is *sociability*, ranging from high sociability (gregarious) to low sociability (avoiding social situations).

Positive Emotionality

As just mentioned, this higher-order dimension refers to the *capacity* of an individual to experience and be involved in the excitement and stimulation of life. This capacity is intrinsically tied to the individual's inherent pre-set for positive emotionality and, at its higher end, is described by such words as affectionate, friendly, optimistic, happy, smiling, cooperative, and considerate.

The sub-categories include:

High Sociability—meaning enjoying and appreciating the company of others. The more sociable a person is, the more that person finds the responsiveness and attention of others to be rewarding. Social children prefer to play with others rather than by themselves, are more responsive to social situations, are friendlier, and want and seek company more often. They prefer to play interactive games in which there is considerable give and take and are more willing to be tolerant of others in order to maintain social contact. When left alone, they often complain that there is nothing for them to do.

Low Sociability—meaning withdrawing and avoiding contact with others. Children with a tendency toward low sociability tend to prefer to play more solitary games and are less responsive to social cues or pressures. They generally spend more time at home and avoid or do not seek peer interactions.

Dominance—referring to the ability to exert an influence over others. Children on the positive end of this personality trait have a capacity for leadership and are able to act cooperatively and competitively in achieving a desirable goal. They are able to be organized, are assertive and forceful, tend to be outspoken, and are referred to as someone who gets things done. Children on the lower range are seen as followers, tend to be more dependent, and tend to yield to others.

Negative Emotionality

This broad higher-order dimension refers to an individual's propensity to experience such feelings as fear, anger, sadness, apprehension, anxiety, and generalized distress. It shows in behaviors like restlessness, wariness, anger, being difficult, depressed, impulsive, and a having a predisposition to later phobic reactions. It is also connected to being vulnerable to experience the adverse effects of stress.

Negative emotionality seems to be a contributing factor for individuals who experience less successful social functioning and who have some difficulty feeling sympathy or empathy for others. The results of recent studies suggest that as the child matures, negative emotionality increasingly manifests as two distinct traits, one tapping into emotions such as fear, worry, and distress; and one that taps into anger and irritability.

Aggressiveness is found in those children who tend to deal with their feelings of anger by responding with physical and/ or verbal attacks. Individual differences in aggressiveness show strong stability by middle childhood with boys showing a consistent and observable level of aggression as early as preschool. Although we usually associate aggressiveness with boys, recent studies have shown that girls express their aggressiveness through "relational aggression," which includes gossiping and social exclusion.

Pro-social dispositions are those behaviors that express the opposite of aggressiveness. Children in this category are described as considerate, helpful, cooperative, generous, and protective of others. They exhibit high levels of empathy and are able to recognize and respond to the feelings of others. Pro-social tendencies are related to higher social functioning and are manifested by greater popularity and social competency.

Constraint-Conscientiousness

This broad higher-order dimension relates to the ability to control, monitor, and modulate one's behavior. It includes responsiveness to social controls, self-restraint, and self-discipline. In its positive range, it is expressed by being able to cope with stress, delay gratification, be self-motivated, and stay focused. In its negative end, it is seen in various forms of impulsive behaviors and poor inhibition. The sub-categories include:

Persistence, which allows a child to focus on a task and to complete it in spite of external distractions and boredom. The positive end of this personality dimension is often associated with academic achievement, while the negative end can resemble behavior usually associated with an attention-deficit disorder.

Mastery/achievement is described as a personality trait that, when at the high range, describes individuals who are curious and interested in the world around them. These are children who experience pleasure in overcoming obstacles, mastering their environments, and who choose challenging tasks over easy ones. They also seem to be able to better cope with failure. The opposite is true of those in the lower end of the range.

Control/impulsive refers to behaviors that range from being careful and able to control and inhibit one's behavior to responding with little or no caution and control. The lower-end group includes such behavior as acting quickly with little thought as to the consequences, difficulty waiting one's turn, and not being able to restrain from talking when inappropriate. There is some evidence that, separate from impulsive behavior, some children are drawn toward excitement-seeking or risk-taking activities.

Activity Level

This category refers to the customary level of physical movement, energy, vigor, and speed expended by an individual and is particularly salient in describing children. Words used to describe high-energy children include bouncing, hopping, whirling, swinging, kicking, and tumbling. They play harder, move faster, talk louder, yell more often, and have more endurance. They also tend to become frustrated and restless when confined and need additional transition time to unwind. Conversely, low-energy children are described as quiet, patient, slow-moving, content, dawdling, drowsy, and "poky." They tend to prefer less vigorous games and sports, are more limited in their endurance, and often require extra time to complete a task.

Agreeableness

Traits on the positive end of agreeableness are described by such words as appreciative, generous, kind, trusting, sympathetic, sincere, and straightforward. On the negative end, it is seen in behaviors that are described as selfish, rude, mistrustful, uncooperative, and hostile. There appears to be a strong correlation between this dimension and positive emotionality, with each reinforcing the other in both positive and negative ranges.

Openness to experience at the high end of the range taps into the capacity for imagination, creativity, intellectual curiosity, insightfulness, and receptivity to inner feelings. Conversely, the lower end would be described by such words as shallow, dense, uninterested, and imperceptive.

The potential for positive or negative interactions between the child and his or her parent is rooted in these temperament/ personality traits. For example, a high-activity child and a high-activity parent will have a different experience of each other than a high-activity child and a low-activity parent or a low-activity child and a high-activity parent. You will find a more detailed discussion of this interaction factor in a later chapter.

In general, individuals at either extreme end of a personality dimension can experience problems associated with that extreme. This is fairly easy to see when one is dealing with the negative end, e.g., very aggressive, painfully shy, not thinking of consequences. But being at the high boundaries of the positive end can also present problems. A too-sociable child may be unduly influenced by peers. A too-controlled child may be unable to be appropriately spontaneous. A child with too much energy may have difficulty in situations requiring extended quiet time. What is the significance of these intrinsic temperament traits and emotional natures in the context of survival systems?

Individuals who need to develop a system will respond to the demands of their environment in keeping with their inherent personality and emotional style. One child, responding to living in a "war zone," builds a tank to defend himself, while another becomes invisible.

In some cases, like the story of Mark and his need to be a "second-banana," a survival system is not solely the result of the child responding to the environment, but more importantly, is a result of a child responding to a belief that adaptation is necessary due to a hidden "individuality" factor. In these systems, the "demand of the environment" is not the primary reason for the adaptation.

The environment played some role, but it is some characteristic in the nature of the individual, and the beliefs attached to those characteristics, that acts as the primary force for the system.

CHAPTER SEVEN

Recognizing Your Uniqueness

POINTS TO MAKE
ACTIONS TO TAKE

Point: Recognizing the unique characteristics that define you is crucial when trying to understand the meaning and purpose of your "custom-made" survival system. There were elements in Mark's environment that could cause a child to experience some later difficulties as an adult. These include his father's unavailability, his grandmother's chronic crises, his awareness of the burdens placed upon his mother, and his empathy for his older brother. I would also include the early negative biases he experienced toward homosexuality. It is doubtful, however, that these factors alone would have been so powerful as to cause him to so diminish his potential. Neither the demands of the environment or the interaction between Mark and his surroundings would have warranted as strong a need for adaptation. Such elements of individuality as Mark's attractive physical appearance, his innate talent, intelligence, his empathetic and sensitive nature, and his early awareness

environment + personality determine survival system

of his homosexuality were primary factors in his emerging survival system of "needing not to be too much."

Action: With new objectivity, take a look at yourself in a mirror and observe what you see and your reaction to that reflection. As in Mark's case, there are both external factors (his good looks, height, thick eyelashes) and internal factors (his creative and performing abilities, intelligence, sociability) that play out in any system. Are your reactions to your reflection positive or negative? If negative, are you looking at yourself through the distorted vision of someone else or someone else's requirement that you not be true to who you are? This would be your responding to the demands of your environment. It could also be that you are looking at yourself through *your* distorted vision based on *your* distorted beliefs.

Point: Don't jump to conclusions based on what *appears* to be an obvious problem. It would have been a waste of time and effort if Mark and I had focused solely on the issue of his being homosexual. The connection between his homosexuality and his survival system lay not in his unawareness of it and not in his experiencing derision because of it. Mark's distorted and prejudiced beliefs of what it *meant* to be gay, based on books, movies, and flamboyant gay men, were major factors fueling his fear of being too much. As he was able to reassess his views, being gay became increasingly acceptable and preferable.

Action: Hold up that mirror again to reflect the inner "you." Listen for echoes of such criticisms as: "I wish you weren't so shy," or "Why aren't you more friendly, like your sister?" or "Can't you ever walk slowly?" How often did you hear someone say, "You're just too sensitive?" By looking at these reflections again, you will be able to change the idea that because there was something "wrong," it had to be *you* who was wrong or *you* who was defective.

We often have negative feelings about ourselves because of negative misinterpretations of and reactions to our innate temperament and emotional nature. Perhaps you might discover as one woman did, that her difficulty with slow-moving activities and people was not because she was intolerant. It was tied to her being born with a very high-activity level.

Point: Your survival system is based on what you believed was the truth. In Mark's case, his belief as to the nature of gay men, based on the distorted portrayals he had seen in movies, television, and theater, was a crucial part of his need for a system.

Sometimes what appears to be a "truth" can ultimately become a prison. To understand how this occurs, we borrow a concept from Formal Logic called a syllogism. When used correctly, a syllogism acts as a formula for being able to draw valid conclusions from known facts. It is made up of two statements, or premises, both assumed to be true. It is the relationship of the first premise (the basic premise) to the second one that determines whether the derived conclusion is correct. The formula for being able to reach a valid conclusion is:

$a = b$ (basic premise)

$c = a$ (premise #2)

Therefore: $c = b$ (valid conclusion)

The syllogism that you may have learned in school goes:

All men (a) are mortal (b) ($a = b$)

Socrates (c) is a man (a) ($c = a$)

Therefore Socrates (c) is mortal (b) ($c = b$)

Basic premises are established through observation. Because we can observe that all men who have ever lived have died, we can conclude that all men are mortal. This is called inductive reasoning. We gather information about our individual worlds and establish basic premises through inductive reasoning.

Once a premise is set, we behave as if it were true. The validity of a conclusion may be questioned, but the truth of the basic premise is rarely challenged.

Basic Premise

Inductive Reasoning   **Deductive Reasoning**

Here's an exaggerated syllogism that could create the need for a survival system:

Rose's father abuses her mother, her grandfather beats her grandmother, her uncles are mean to their wives, and her brother takes advantage of her. Through her observations, she concludes a basic premise that all men are brutes. This now becomes a basic truth of her life. Without conscious awareness of her basic premise, she reasons that:

All men are brutes;

John, my boyfriend, is a man;

Therefore John must be a brute.

No wonder Rose has trouble establishing a relationship with a man. If the basic premise was changed to "Some men are brutes" she could not necessarily conclude that John is in that group of men who are brutes.

You can see how, in Mark's case, a false basic premise became a powerful factor in his survival system.

His syllogism went: All gay men are too much; I'm a gay man; Therefore, I must be too much.

Action: Put your beliefs into the form of syllogisms. Analyze not only the validity of your conclusions, but especially the truth of your premises. You may discover false premises that still influence your feelings and behaviors. You may also learn that conclusions based on the truths of your childhood are no longer valid.

Point: We all have memories that continue to elicit strong emotional reactions. But when a memory appears to be unimportant, yet continues to create an internal upheaval, take another look. An example is Mark's memory of the teacher's comments about his long, thick lashes being wasted on a boy. On the surface it seemed like a benign comment, but Mark's emotional reaction recalling that memory was very strong. So strong, that we had our first clue as to his underlying fear of being too much.

Another possible clue is a memory that usually elicits a strong reaction in most people but causes little or no emotional reaction in you. Frank's casual recalling of his father leaving and giving him the responsibility of his mother and sisters is such a memory. You will find many examples of discrepancies between memory and reaction as you read the various case histories.

Action: Pay close attention to your reactions as you recall events from your past. Do you overreact to a seemingly benign memory? Conversely, do you not react to a recalled event and wonder if your lack of reaction is appropriate? You may not understand the significance of these discrepancies immediately, but hold on to them and note them as possible clues.

Point: A powerful tool for understanding and changing the reality that exists between individuals is to be found in "the space-between." In Mark's case, it allowed us to see how he projected his biased beliefs into the space-between us, and then experienced them as coming from me. Paying close attention to the distortions being created in the reality of the space-between us allowed him to recognize and change his internal belief system.

One way of understanding the meaning of the "space-between" is that in any interaction there are two or more people with a certain amount of space existing between them, creating what we call "the space-between." This "space" holds verbal language—what is said and what is not said—body language, *vibe* emotions, beliefs, the moment-to-moment experiencing, the positives and/or negatives, the "feel" of the interaction that includes the explicit and implicit material existing in each of the individuals involved and which, overtly and covertly, gets communicated by them. The sum total of all of this creates a certain quality in the interaction resulting in the "space-between."

An example of this concept is the "space-between" in the theater, which refers to the kind of reality the actors are creating in any given scene. When a scene is not working and/or not conveying the playwright's intent, the director attempts to change the "feel" of that space. The director may seem to be working with individual actors, but his focus is on helping the actors change what is being played out between them. The closer the actors get to conveying the meaning of the play in the space between them, the more the audience will experience "the reality" the writer had intended. There is also a "space-between" the performing actors on the stage and the audience. Unlike the movies where performances, once filmed are unchangeable, theater performances—dependent on the differing audiences each night and the chemistry created by the interaction of the actors and audience—can offer subtle, variable versions of the play.

Action: Let's take this concept and see how it can be used by you to change your reality. Each time you interact with another, a series of "space-betweens" is created, not unlike the unfolding scenes in a play. In these "plays" however, you become the actor, director, and audience. The more you become aware of the kind of reality you and the other(s) are creating, the more the distortions in that reality can come to the surface. And the more you catch the distortions in the "space-between," particularly those that are the ones you have been caught in, the more power you have to create a different reality.

It may be helpful to take another look at how Mark and I used the "space-between" to change his survival system. The initial awareness of the distortion in our "space-between" was mine, based on my sense that Mark was acutely aware of my reactions to him and of me as a person. My sense that something felt different with Mark was based on a comparison with how other patients related to me. The "space-between" soon offered information about how he assumed that I, the other, shared the same distortions and biases he had internalized. In each case, my discomfort with what he was projecting on me offered a clue as to what was happening between us. It also offered Mark an opportunity to understand and change two distorted ways he related; his internalized bias about homosexuality distorting how he related to himself, and how his sensitivity to another was being incorrectly used to distort an interaction with another in "the space-between."

To maximize the use of the "space-between" concept, keep in mind that you need to play three separate roles.

As one of the actors, you must be aware of what you are putting into the "space-between."

As the audience, you must recognize the reality that is being created. If that reality is not what you want or mean to create, you may: (a) unknowingly be creating a false or distorted reality; (b) you have a clue as to what the other person might be putting into that space.

As the director, you work toward creating the kind of reality you want. In some cases it is important to recognize that the "play" is going to fail and that you may need to do some reshuffling or recasting of "actors."

It is important then to pay attention to what you are feeling and what "vibrations" you are picking up when relating to the others in the "space-between." Your reaction to the reality being created in that space offers valuable clues to such questions as: if a specific interaction feels different than other interactions under similar circumstances, is the difference due to you or the others; if you are experiencing feelings of resentment, guilt, confusion, anger or sadness, are they in reaction to what the other person is silently or verbally playing out; or is the other inappropriately reacting to what you are putting in the space-between.

Start to sensitize yourself to the "feel" of the space between you and the other in easy interactions with neutral others. As you gain more insight into how and why the reality gets distorted, either by you or the other, practice various strategies for achieving the reality you want. When ready, move on to more difficult interactions with more difficult others, and see if, by working in the "space-between," you can create a new, more desirable and permanent reality for yourself. Richard Buckminster Fuller captured this when he said: "You never change things by fighting the existing reality. To change something, build a new model that makes the existing model obsolete."

CHAPTER EIGHT

Environmental Demands of Childhood

A myth existed for many centuries that children were not affected by traumas, even as powerful a one as war. Or, if they were, they surely left any trace of their negative experiences behind in childhood. That myth was finally broken, and the power of an early trauma to affect an individual is now widely accepted. What is overlooked, however, is the degree to which less obviously traumatic environments in which a child exists can subtly influence and hamper the future psychological growth of that child, and the adult that child becomes. The following chapters relating to the environment of your childhood offer a series of case histories illustrating survival systems developed in response to a number of difficult environments.

The environment of your childhood is the physical, psychological, and sociological matrix into which you were born. Its influence operates on two levels. The first is the observable, external world including such variables as: where you live, your parents' physical health, their psychological stability, their physical and/or emotional availability, their parenting skills, any patterns of addiction, your family's ethnic or racial background, socioeconomic class, and financial stability. Included among external factors as well are: your birth order, your relationship with your siblings, not having any siblings, the presence or absence of significant relatives, important family friends, and the positive and/or negative influences of people who might have been part of your life.

The second level holds what I call the "vibrations" of the environment, including both explicit and implicit communications. These verbal and non-verbal messages, often from a parent, are hidden within family interactions. Remember, implicit knowing is "relational" knowing, non-consciously knowing how to be with the other. As such, these vibrations are powerful forces able to create greater disruptions than more obvious dynamics. An example of an environmental vibration would be the narcissism of Snow White's stepmother and her need to be the fairest of them all, resonating as a danger. Snow White's non-conscious response is to become ugly in order to avoid a dangerous reaction. These hidden messages act to influence how we feel and behave, for like buried wires that carry power to run our machines, they act as underground "emotional wires" to run our lives.

Certain childhood environments are more likely to require a survival adaptation. For example, we don't often see our childhood in the context of a war zone—an environment that does not respect a child's integrity and boundaries. Certainly, any child who was subjected to physical, sexual, emotional, or verbal abuse was living in a war zone.

War zones require protective adaptations. Some children build solid tanks around themselves, equipped with all the trappings of a tank, to enable them to experience themselves as invulnerable and untouchable. They tend to stay within that tank and avoid contact with others. Unfortunately, the tanks do not have escape hatches. The child, now an adult, leaves the war zone of childhood and is trapped in a tank of isolation and invulnerability.

Another adaptation to a war zone is one of disappearing into the walls—"if you can't see me, you can't shoot me." The child becomes invisible and thus escapes attacks. But the child, now an adult, is caught in patterns of obscurity and is an individual who is invariably ignored, forgotten, and overlooked.

Bevin, fourteen years old, is an example of a child caught in the warfare between his parents. He was referred for counseling because of his disruptive behavior in school and a threat of expulsion. I decided to include his parents in our sessions, hoping to cut through his acting-out behavior quickly. His parents were enraged and disgusted with him and spent most of the sessions berating their son. Hoping to get more information about Bevin's younger years as well as a sense of the family unit, I encouraged his parents to talk about themselves. Answering my question of, "What made you two decide to get married?" both parents turned toward Bevin and, with anger and resentment in their voices, said "him." Fifteen years after Bevin's mother had gotten pregnant at seventeen, both parents were still blaming him for their having "had" to get married. Bevin, reacting to the negative vibrations directed at him, had developed a pattern of being the "bad boy." This pattern not only expressed his unhappiness, but more importantly offered him an explanation as to why his parents didn't like him.

Another environment that holds powerful demands is one that includes a parent's own archaic survival system. *Depending on their own history, temperament and life experiences, parents bring to the interactions with their children their own dysfunctional "needs" that once met their childhood survival requirements.* The wicked Queen's need to be the "fairest of them all" was there for everyone to see. But what about the parent who is "good," yet caught in a damaging system. To illustrate this point, let's make up an exaggerated story of a good mother, Mary, and how her hidden survival "need" might act as an "environmental demand" on her children.

Our Mary was a disappointment from the beginning, the third girl in the family, born two years after her twin sisters. Both parents had hoped for a son and were overjoyed when their fourth child, a boy, was born a year later. Mary felt she was unimportant to the family, and in some ways, she was right. After all, her sisters were special because they were first-born and twins. Her younger brother was special just because he was a boy. Mary felt that there was nothing special about her, and she questioned whether she belonged or was welcome in the family. Reacting to what she believed were her family's feelings toward her, as well as the negative feelings she had about herself, Mary established her importance by becoming the good and responsible child. She was the one who was always available to do whatever her parents or siblings wanted her to do; and, as she grew, she became the one member of the family who was essential to the family's functioning. In the language of this book, Mary grew up with a survival need of "needing to be needed." Her "need to be needed" was pervasive, spreading into all facets of her life, so that her world was limited ultimately to people who would need her. Thus, her sense of her own existence depended, not on her intrinsic worth, but on her worth in relation to what she could do for another.

Mary grows up, gets married, and has children. Her need to be needed is a non-conscious, hidden facet of her functioning. She is seen as a wonderful mother, a woman devoted to her family who is essential and invaluable to their well-being. What impact can Mary's survival system have on her children? A mother who has a "need to be needed" sends powerful messages: that the child can function only with the help of the mother; that life is too difficult for this child and he or she must depend on others; and that, "if you want me to love you, you must need me." Her children react to this environmental demand in their own characteristic ways. They become, perhaps, individuals who remain dependent on others. Or conversely, people who develop their own systems of needing to remain aloof from others for fear of becoming "dependent" on them.

My first experience with adaptation to a powerful dysfunctional need occurred during my internship at a clinic while still a graduate student. My new assignment was as co-leader of a group of women who had been brought to the court's attention for child abuse or neglect. The group, under the direction of an experienced therapist, consisted of eight young, single mothers and their thirteen children who were all under the age of five. The group's reputation as the clinic's most difficult and chaotic was well established. Some members had required psychiatric hospitalizations during the previous year, and all had the therapist's home phone number, which they called freely, day or night.

A week after I was introduced to the group, the clinic called to tell me that the senior therapist had died, having informed no one that she had been under treatment for terminal cancer. I was asked to help the mothers deal with her death and, in the process, they bonded to me and became my group and my responsibility.

I met regularly with the mothers, expecting each day to be drowned in a tidal wave of disaster. But nothing happened—no phone calls at home, no need to hospitalize anyone, no chaos. Why would a group that had been difficult, needy, demanding, "out-of-control," and resistant to change suddenly stop all such behaviors? I knew it could not be because of my therapeutic skills—I was still in training.

Trying to understand what had caused such a drastic change, I remembered reading about the heiress to the Winchester rifle fortune. She kept making additions to her home—staircases that went nowhere, doors that opened up to blank spaces, rooms that could not be used. The myth was that Mrs. Winchester was caught in the fantasy that she would not die as long as her house remained unfinished. I believe the group's prior therapist had had a similar fantasy. As long as the group desperately needed her, she would not die. The group had responded by acting out that desperate need, and their own growth and change became secondary. They had been like the Winchester house—going nowhere, remaining "unfinished." But then I came along, and I did not need them to need me.

Most psychologists believe that the therapist/patient relationship can be likened to the parent/child relationship. It is not that the therapist sees the patient as a child, but rather that the nature of the relationship gives the therapist an authoritative influence not unlike that of a parent. If a group could adapt to the powerful needs of a therapist, could not a child adapt to the powerful needs of a parent?

Because survival systems are developed in childhood, it is essential that you recognize and understand the external and internal factors of your early environment from a child's point of view. Your belief that you needed a survival system would have been based on you, as a child, interpreting the behaviors and attitudes of the adults in your world. The adult Snow White from "A Tale of Survival" might realize that she had suffered the loss of her parents as well as having to deal with a very difficult stepmother. Thinking as an adult, it is unlikely that she would have arrived at her original seven-year-old solution. Imagining herself a child thinking concretely, her "need to be ugly" would be more obvious.

When parents continue to have unresolved, internalized issues, they unwittingly affect their children in ways that can be as damaging as the wicked Queen in the Snow White story. The five stories that follow explore a child's response to the silent signals of danger vibrating from a "magic mirror" and the manifestations of that response in that child, as an adult.

The first case history is of a parent's distorted belief as to the nature of the world. A discrepancy between the inner belief of the parent and the current reality in which the parent and child exist, may lead the child to assume a survival system that belongs to the parent's past. The second case is of a parent's inappropriate belief as to the nature of parenting.

The next two cases of a child needing a survival system relate to family secrets and family myths. Family secrets distort a child's environment because the family needs to hide a reality they find upsetting or shameful. Family myths distort the environment because of a need to pretend that a reality doesn't exist.

The final case history is one about distortions in family power.

In all the histories given, a key question asked over and over again was: "Whose needs got met?" This is a question you will find yourself asking in relation to your history.

CHAPTER NINE

Parents' Beliefs as to the Nature of the World

S oon after receiving my graduate degree, I was hired as a counselor in a private school for children with emotional problems. My experience with James, a ten-year-old boy who had not spoken since he was five, is the most dramatic example of how a discrepancy between the inner beliefs of the parent and the actual, current reality within which the parent and the child live, can impact the child. The child can get a covert, coded message of survival that, in actuality, belongs to the inner, past world of the parent.

The Need to Be Silent: James

James had stopped speaking when he started kindergarten. His teachers believed at first that he was shy. The explanation for his silence soon shifted to a possible learning disorder. But this idea was dropped after it became clear that James was absorbing information in class and doing well on written examinations. Although no one could answer the question of why James didn't speak, it was obvious that his continued silence was beginning to affect his work in school, as well as isolating him from the other children. He was placed in a Special Education class with the hope that a smaller class size and increased teacher involvement would break through his silence. It did not. After several semesters, it was recommended that he be transferred to a private school that offered help for children with emotional problems. He arrived there a year before I did.

The school records showed that an extensive psychological examination failed to uncover any major emotional traumas, and James was diagnosed as a "self-selected mute, cause unknown." Two things were noted in the records: first, the father was the only person James had continued to speak to over these years of silence but only in the privacy of their home (the parents were divorced and James lived with the father). And second, James avoided any contact, including eye contact, with others. Both he and his father had been in counseling the previous year, the boy with a senior therapist and the father in a parenting group. In spite of weekly therapy sessions and meetings with speech specialists, the boy continued to be mute.

The case was assigned to me with the suggestion that I see the father and son together. It seemed to me that the school wasn't sure what to do with this family and did not want an experienced therapist assigned, for another year, to a case they saw as having limited possibilities for change. My being so new to the profession made my time less "wasteful" if there was no improvement. The leader of the parenting group also had reported that, although the father seemed to be committed to the group, the group knew little about him as he had kept himself apart from the other parents and had not talked about himself or his son.

And so the father, James, and I met, with the events of that first meeting setting the tone for what would follow for the next year and a half.

The father walked into my room, anxiously looked around, expressed his concern for his son's condition and sat down in one of the three chairs I had carefully arranged in order to facilitate communication among us. James slowly followed his father into the room, his head down, shoulders slumped, furtively looked around and quickly picked up the third chair, moving it to a distant corner of the room. So much for easy communication! I had no idea what approach would be effective with James, but I knew that challenging him about moving the chair was not wise at that early introductory stage; and I decided to take a more prudent approach. I ignored James, focusing instead on his father.

The early sessions were difficult for all of us, and I can still feel the discomfort of the long silences. The father, who was born and raised in Southeast Asia, was hesitant to talk about himself; and I was reluctant to ask too many questions that he might find unnerving. James sat silently in the corner.

"How long have you been in this country?" I asked.

"A long time," he answered, followed by a long silence.

"How long were you and your wife married?" I asked.

"Not very long," he answered, followed by a long silence.

"Do you have any idea why James doesn't speak?" I asked.

"No," he answered—another long silence.

And so it went.

Over time I began to realize that the father did not fully understand English. He had learned to cover up this deficiency by appearing to understand what was being said, without actually getting the full meaning and subtlety of the conversation.

No wonder he is so guarded, I thought. He's not always sure what I'm asking and why I'm asking it. I began to be more specific in my questions and shared my belief that "English is a very difficult language to learn."

He, in turn, realized that I was making an effort to better communicate with him, that I wasn't judging him, and that I seemed to be genuinely interested in helping him and his son. A bond began to form between us.

He hesitantly began to tell me his life story. He was born into an affluent Asian family. When he was twelve, the Japanese army invaded his country; and he was interned in a concentration camp, separated from his family. He remained in the camp until the war ended. He was then seventeen and, returning to his homeland, found that his family had left because of the political unrest that followed the end of the war. When I asked if he had been able to find them, all he would say was that he had tracked them to Europe. His silence about his family's whereabouts appeared to be connected to a major disagreement he had had with them. He decided that the United States offered more opportunity, and he eventually was able to emigrate to this country.

During our weekly meetings, James continued to sit in the far corner of the room, silent, his head bowed. After several unsuccessful attempts to make contact with him, I elected to continue to ignore him and stayed focused on his father. Somehow these meetings were having an effect on James, as his teacher reported to me that he had begun to say a few tentative words in class. At the time, I had no idea why.

The father continued to share his story. "I met my wife soon after I came to this country," he told me. "She was a pretty girl, vcry young, maybe too young to get married and have a child. Anyway, she left me when James was three or four."

I asked him if James ever saw his mother.

"Yes," he answered. "Once in a while. She has her own family now."

I asked him if he had met anyone else.

"No, no," he answered, rather emphatically. "No time for that sort of thing."

It was clear that the father was totally alone, isolated, had no family and had almost no contact with others aside from some limited associations with co-workers.

James continued to sit in the far corner of the room, still silent, still with his head bowed, still making no contact with me.

But the reports coming back to me from others in weekly staff meetings said that he was now beginning to put sentences together, to actually talk in class; and I was getting the credit for breaking his silence. During one staff meeting, the director of the school complimented me on the good work I was doing with a difficult case. I had to sheepishly admit that I hadn't a clue as to why James was now talking or what he felt or thought.

"James never speaks to me," I confessed. "He sits at the other end of the room, doesn't participate, and says nothing, nothing at all. In fact," I further confessed, "I ignore him and only talk to his father." I did add, however, that I was learning a lot about the father.

There was general agreement that the answer to why James had begun to speak was important, but what really mattered more was that he was talking. Obviously, something of significance was going on in our sessions.

Over the months, the father continued to share his story. At first, it was about his post-Asia life: his journey to the States, his move to California, his marriage and divorce, learning his trade, his work, his current problems, his concern for his son's future. Then he started to talk about growing up in the country of his birth: his family's history going back several generations, stories about his mother and father and his two brothers, about what his life was like in a wealthy family, about what life was like before the terrible war. Every once in a while I would see James' eyes grow large with wonder, and I knew that he had never heard these stories before. Although he still sat in the corner, never saying a word, he was now talking freely in class. In fact, he was beginning to talk too much in class.

"Could you please talk to James about his talking," his teacher requested one day. "I don't want to discourage him, but he needs to understand when talking is appropriate and when it's not."

I would try, I told her, but I suggested that she too explain it since I wasn't sure that James took me very seriously. I was wrong about that, as I was to learn later.

"I was very lucky," the father said one day, after we had been meeting for over a year. "I was not damaged by being in that camp. I managed to eat, to work hard, to stay out of the way, and not get into trouble. Some of the boys did not do so good." He spoke quietly and unemotionally. It was the first time he made any mention of his experiences in the concentration camp.

The senior therapist, who was acting as my consultant and who had been closely monitoring the case, encouraged me to go into this new territory, but very carefully and gently.

"He had to have been damaged by his experiences," he said. "There just may be a connection between that and James." And he was right. The pieces of the puzzle began to fit together as the father continued to tell me what were to him minor episodes of the camp's routine, "insignificant" stories about the guards and "throw-away" memories of the other children. He showed little emotion when he remembered a long-forgotten event or when he touched upon some experience of camp life. But I felt that beneath his unperturbed exterior was a seething cauldron of emotions. He never gave details and I never asked for more, but it was clear that he had been molded by the world of the concentration camp. What was also clear was that he had never talked about it to anyone before.

One theme that emerged over and over again was how the elder men of the camp had tried to protect the children by guiding and counseling them. For the five years he was in the camp, the elders had preached to each child: *Your survival depends on not being seen. Your survival depends on not bringing any attention to yourself. You must not talk. You must not make eye contact, for the wrong word or look will be considered a challenge and you must not challenge them. Keep your head down—it is safer that way. Keep to yourself, for they see conspiracy in every corner. They are powerful and dangerous. But listen to us and you will survive.*

There it was. The father's inner world had been formed and shaped by the dangers of a concentration camp and the warnings of the elders. His continued and profound isolation by a language barrier, by his distrust of people, by his fear of loss and abandonment as a result of so many losses, had reinforced the power and horror of the camp. The children of the camp had been taught that survival depended on not bringing attention to oneself, on not talking, on not challenging, and on not making eye-contact with others. This was the "vibration" that James had learned from his father, and this was exactly what James had been doing—except that he was not the one living in a concentration camp.

What allowed James to speak was the change in the vibrations and implicit communications from his father, ultimately allowing James a different experience of "how to be" in the world. The boy had never seen or heard his father relate to another person in any trusting way. James had played out his father's powerful concentration camp belief system until he was exposed, in that room, to his father's changing internal world.

James was outgrowing the school and needed to move on to junior high school. The administrators believed that he would be better served by continuing to attend in a private school with programs that would meet his special needs. James didn't believe that he still had "special needs" and had expressed to his teacher his desire to return to his neighborhood school and become "one of the regular guys."

Why was James talking to everyone else, particularly his teacher, whom he dearly loved, and never to me? James saw me as very powerful—after all, I had changed his father. The powerful ones in the internalized world of the father were not the elders, but the enemy. And James was not taking any chances.

His teacher agreed that he would be fine in regular classes. The administration wasn't sure and their decision rested on my recommendation. I thought it was crucial that I hear what James had to say; and, to be honest, I sensed it might be my only chance to get him to talk directly to me. So James and I took a walk around the grounds. I explained to him that his teacher reported that his desire was to go to his neighborhood school, that she supported his wish, but that I needed him to tell me what he wanted. I waited. He remained silent, still keeping his head down and still avoiding any contact with me.

I stopped walking and turned to him. "Okay, James," I said, "do you want to go back to regular school?"

His head came up. He looked me in the eye and said, "Yes!" Then he turned and quickly walked away.

That one word was the only thing he ever said to me.

CHAPTER TEN

Parents' Belief as to the Nature of Parenting

O ne may be nearing the traditional age of retirement and still be trapped in a survival system. But it's never too late to uncover the underlying beliefs that cause one to remain "stuck."

The Need to Stay Untouched: Len

Len was in his late sixties when he was referred to me by his doctor. He had been diagnosed with a mild heart condition that his doctor believed was being exacerbated by stress and internalized tension. Len also reported experiencing recent unexpected and unexplained short episodes of rage that were not in keeping with his usual demeanor. He was receptive to the idea of therapy, and we agreed to set weekly sessions for the next several months.

Our early meetings went well as I learned the basics of his background. He was raised in a small town, the only child in a traditional family, his father an executive in the local power plant, his mother staying home to care for him. He was particularly fond of his father although the demands on his father had not left much time for father/son activities. He could recall no major family upheavals, no traumas, and no serious problems through his school years and beyond. In his mid-twenties he had married a girl he had met in college. They had two children, now both grown.

Len had been an account executive in advertising for many years, eventually becoming a partner in the firm. I could understand why he had been so successful. He was affable, agreeable, and had an ability to make people feel that he was truly available to them. He had recently retired. And at first, I thought that his tension and anger were tied to his being forced to end his professional career. It soon became clear, however, that he enjoyed his new freedom, for he had always wanted to be an artist and had set up a studio in his garage. He was now taking art classes several times a week and had recently participated in a group show at a local gallery.

As our sessions continued, the picture Len was sketching started to shift. He appeared comfortable and at ease as he shared his life story, filled with people and activities; but there was a vibration in our "space-between" that signaled that something else was going on. Although I could not identify exactly what I was picking up, it seemed to be tied to loneliness and isolation. It's usually not too difficult to identify individuals struggling with isolation when they are obviously not connected to others, but this pattern did not seem to fit Len. On the surface, he appeared to have many involvements—with family, friends, his new art world, and so on. What was I sensing that was so elusive?

I began to recognize that an invisible glass wall surrounded Len, leaving him untouched and untouchable. I shared my image of this imaginary barrier with Len; and although surprised that I had sensed it, he did not deny its existence. He also did not deny the loneliness he had felt for most of his life and his unsuccessful struggle to make contact with others. Here then was the possible telltale sign of a survival system—a discrepancy between what he wanted to have and what he may have needed not to have.

I asked him if his invisible wall existed within his family.

"If you mean by invisible wall," he replied, "that I feel a sense of isolation in my family, then yes. But I don't know if it's my wall or my family's lack of involvement with me. My wife's law practice keeps her physically and emotionally occupied. And although I was close to my kids when they were young, they have gone on to have their own lives, quite separate from mine."

Over the years I've generally been able to make contact with people who were difficult to reach, but it appeared increasingly likely that Len was going to be a more difficult case. No matter what route I took trying to reach him, including talking about his glass wall and interpreting the possible reasons for its existence, he stayed behind it.

And then we had a breakthrough. I had just returned from a trip during which I had seen a major exhibit of the paintings of Matisse. Knowing Len's interest in art, I casually mentioned how much I had enjoyed the exhibit. Len immediately responded, and we began a discussion of the work of this artist. I could feel our "space-between" begin to change during that session; and I knew that I had, at last, found a route to reach him. It was obvious that Len, too, felt the shift in our interaction.

"I guess it's safe to talk about art," Len said, "because I can feel myself poking holes in my wall."

I asked him why he thought our talking about art allowed him to lower his guard. "I'm not sure," he said. "But it feels more neutral."

Neutral against what, I wondered.

Our sessions became centered on themes relating to the world of art. Fortunately for our work, I have had a hobby of visiting major art exhibits all over the country and I was able to share those experiences with Len. He, in response, increasingly invited me to enter his world. Slowly the glass wall between us began to dissolve.

One day, Len came to a session with some of his smaller charcoal drawings and oils. His work was a reflection of his inner-self. Most of the canvases were of isolated people, not touching, not making contact with each other or the viewer. There was one oil painting in particular that seemed to capture his loneliness. It was a profile view of a woman sitting alone at a table, her crossed hands barely touching the table's surface, her feet not quite touching the floor. The background was muted and dark; and, in subtle ways, the woman appeared to blend with the nothingness of the painted walls. Only Len's landscapes had a touch of joy and color, but none included any human figures.

Len's physical condition began to improve as his tension eased, and he reported no further episodes of unexplained anger. The dissolving of his glass wall during our meetings was helping him, but he continued to feel its constrictions and limitations. The reasons for his isolation continued to elude us. And I was running out of art exhibits I could share with him.

We were again exploring the theme of loneliness and isolation when I made some comment about how important it was for people to have a sense of involvement. Len misunderstood me and responded with a short story illustrating the theme of intrusion. In my attempt to clarify the point I was making, I put my words into the form of a question instead of a statement.

"What's the difference," I asked, "between intrusion and involvement?"

To my complete surprise, Len answered, "There isn't any."

"You're joking," I said, finding it difficult to believe he had made no distinction.

"No," he answered, "I'm not joking. I don't believe there is a difference."

"No wonder you're so isolated. Not knowing the difference between intrusion and involvement has to be a major source of your needing a glass wall," I said.

Len was as surprised with my response as I was with his. "Well, he asked, "What is the difference?"

I started to define the words, realized that I needed a greater authority to convince Len, and turned to the dictionary.

"To intrude," I read, "is to thrust oneself in without invitation, permission or welcome. Intrusion is an act of intruding. To involve is to include, to engage as a participant."

Len was silent for a long time. "Read that again," he requested. I repeated the definitions and waited for Len to respond. He continued to be silent. I could not begin to guess where his mind had gone.

He broke the silence with, "My father was a very patient man and never wanted others, particularly my mother, to ever be upset. He was always available to anyone who needed him; and it seemed to me, as a young boy, that a lot of people needed him. He was my hero, my idol, the man who was my model for what a man should be. And when my mother would do something that angered me, my father would encourage me not to upset her. 'You're the man,' he would say. 'It's your responsibility to handle it without making her feel bad.' And I would do just that, mainly to please my father and not have him be disappointed in me."

I pursued, oh-so-gently, what kinds of things his mother might do that would have upset or angered him.

"I guess she was just trying to be a good mother or what she believed a good mother was supposed to be. By that I mean that she seemed to need to be in my life in a way that didn't feel right." Len was struggling to explain what he meant. I felt that his father's admonishments to not upset his mother had generalized into his not being able to criticize or say anything negative about her.

I shared with him the concept of the "good-enough mother," the mother who allows her baby to experience his own need, signal, and have his need met. Then I continued with the mother who was particularly difficult to deal with, the mother who wants to be *the good mother*. Her story is one in which baby is content—but convinced that baby is hungry, she offers her breast. I finished my explanation with "Offer a breast to a baby, baby sucks. Whose need got met?"

After a particularly long silence, Len said, "I guess I never told you that my mother was a teacher's aide in every class of mine, through junior high school."

I looked at Len and at first could only shake my head. "No wonder you don't know the difference between intrusion and involvement."

Len's healing began. We spent hours talking about what were appropriate parenting behaviors, exploring those episodes in which mother had unknowingly imposed her needs on him. Len recalled a number of times when he had felt that his mother had seriously intruded into his territory. She checked his room for any suspicious magazines and books, read his mail, reviewed his schoolwork, spoke to the mothers of his friends, and kept a wary eye on all of his comings and goings.

We could only speculate as to why his mother had been so inappropriately involved in his life. But speculation can help by offering understandable explanations for seemingly inexplicable behaviors. Len thought the answer lay in her confusion as to what it meant to be a caring parent. She had no activities other than being his mother, no other outlets for her energy, and a husband who was not very available. Raising her only child, we both came to believe, was her primary mission in life.

It was during one of our discussions about his mother that Len mentioned that he had familiar feelings of intrusion by his wife.

"She's always been rather insensitive to my space," he said. "And her training as a lawyer probably hasn't helped. She's particularly insensitive now when she invades my studio and feels a need to clean it, messing up the order of my disorder."

I asked him if he ever requested she not do that.

His expected reply was, "No, it would only upset her."

As his sessions continued, Len was able to express his sadness at the unavailability of his father and how important it was for him to live up to the "manly" code his father had set. These discussions were a perfect introduction to Len's understanding of the false premises of his childhood. He had formulated his syllogism as: All strong men do not upset other people; I want to be a strong man; Therefore, I must not upset anyone regardless of what they may do.

As he continued to allow himself more access to the memories of his childhood, he began to understand where the real power of his system lay.

"I would have done anything to not disappoint my father," he said one day. "After awhile, it didn't matter what my mother did, I was not going to react."

I agreed that he had trained himself to not react, at least overtly. But I pointed out, he did react internally. His hidden wall was a barrier against her intrusions as well as protection against her recognizing his negative reactions. One of the advantages, Len discovered, to these internal protections was a real talent and ability for handling difficult situations and people. The years of his father's training to not upset others had given him an extra edge in his ability to deal with difficult clients.

At my suggestion, Len looked into the latest parenting literature, even attending a daylong seminar on the subject. Discovering an entirely different approach to healthy parenting allowed him to recognize, understand, and validate many of his earlier negative experiences.

Len began to share some of what he was discovering in our sessions with his wife and had a pleasant, unexpected surprise. She revealed that her unavailability to him was rooted in her belief that he had not been happy with her. She had sensed a void between them and had assumed that it was constructed only as a barrier to keep her out. Her solution in the earlier years had been to fill that void with her own career. But lately, with his retirement and new interest in art, she had felt particularly shut out of his life. Cleaning his studio was her attempt to become more involved with him. By letting down his wall to her, he began to appreciate his wife's desire to be involved in his life instead of experiencing it as intrusive.

Wanting to be a good father, Len had acted in the reverse way of his parents. Not wanting to intrude in his children's lives as they approached adolescence, he had sent a message misinterpreted by them as his not being particularly interested in their lives. Taking courage from his success in sharing his background with his wife, he took a risk by revealing his true emotional history to his children. And again, he was rewarded with positive and supportive responses.

By the end of our sessions, Len was able to dissolve his wall in so far as it related to his immediate family. With their help, he began to open up to others in his world.

And hanging in the corner of my living room is a small oil painting of a woman, ambiguously facing toward, or away, from the viewer, a gift from a former patient.

CHAPTER ELEVEN

Changing the Effects of Parents' Beliefs

POINTS TO MAKE
ACTIONS TO TAKE

Point: Your understanding of the possible traumas experienced by your parents, when they were children, sheds light on why you may have believed that you needed a survival system. James wasn't adapting to the direct vibrations of his environment but rather to the implicit messages inherent in his father's earlier experiences in the concentration camp, as well as his father's parenting style reflective of that experience. These messages were then reinforced by the father's continuing isolation.

Studies of children whose parents had survived the Holocaust showed that these children appeared to have been affected by their parents' traumas. Strong in their belief of what is best for their children, and unknowingly committed to teaching ways of survival, these parents conveyed to their children the life conditions under which they had survived the war. In keeping with the parent's belief that **surviving is the essential core issue** is their fear that the world is an unpredictable place. This, in turn, leads to behaviors requiring a need to be vigilant to deal with such unpredictable possibilities. Parental over-protectiveness, a strong finding in the research, was manifested by strong parental control and rules limiting the child's activities. In a reversal of reactions, the children reported fear of losing or being separated from their parents. What messages of survival were conveyed to the child often depended on what conditions the parent needed to survive. For example, for some parents, survival meant remaining in hiding. These parents were extremely overprotective, resulting in their children tending to be overly dependent. Their children continued to struggle with separation even as adults.

For other survivors, the message they conveyed could be of fighting back, at times expressed by excessive activity to achieve and build. And for others, one could survive by remaining numb.

Recent studies have shown a continuation of the effects of the Holocaust on third-generation children. Results of these studies confirm that children of original survivors, now parents themselves, conveyed similar concerns of survival issues to their children, as well as a general sense of impending danger, a fear of loss, and a fear of separation.

The devastating effect on the internalized world of a parent is not limited to traumas associated with war and concentration camps. The physical, sexual, or emotional abuse of a parent, when that parent was a child, can create a strong internal belief about the abusive nature of people and the world in general. The child of that parent is vulnerable to experiencing the parent's internal reality of abuse and distrust, rather than the current reality in which there is no abuse. The parent who lived through the Great Depression of the 1930s could have internalized a survival belief attached to a lack of resources, leading to a pattern of needing to hoard. Traumas relating to the force of nature—earthquakes, tornadoes, tsunamis, floods—can powerfully affect individuals who, in turn, would convey messages of survival to their future generations. Some research indicates that individuals who are in close contact with survivors of a trauma experience "secondary traumatization." Simply caring deeply about family members makes us emotionally vulnerable to the traumas that affect them. We can become "victims" because of our emotional bond with our traumatized family member.

Action: The first step is to discover the full history of your parents. Any experiences relating to war should be seen as powerful, influencing factors of your childhood. The next step is to understand how your parents reacted to that experience. As we have seen with James, his father's internalizing of the words of the elders to not speak, not make eye contact, and not challenge, echoed in James' behavior. The father's subsequent isolation continued the power of those internalized words. The key to James being able to speak was James experiencing the changing inner world of his father as the father and I spent time establishing a trusting, safe relationship and breaking that wall of isolation. Invaluable to that was the slow, gentle uncovering of the father's history, ultimately changing both of their lives.

Unlike James, who unknowingly changed his behavior in response to the changing vibrations of his father, you will have to take a more conscious and active role. Understanding in what ways your parents reacted to their "war" environments gives you insight into your adaptations. And it offers an opportunity to modify what you had internalized as a distorted sense of the nature of the world and its dangers.

Point: Catching the vibrations that echo in a family when a parent has experienced a previous trauma can be difficult. I learned how elusive those vibrations could be when I worked with a young woman whose father had been a prisoner in a German concentration camp. Although we spent considerable time discussing issues relating to her father, there seemed to be something that we were unable to touch. Neither she nor I, however, had a clue as to what that "something" was.

We discovered the "something" in a two-volume series called *Maus: A Survivor's Tale* by Art Spiegelman. In the first volume, Spiegelman, through the brilliant use of cartoons, described his life with his father, a survivor of a German concentration camp. In the second book, again using cartoons, Spiegelman captured the horror of the camp experience. A friend had recommended the books to my patient who, in turn, told me about her strong reaction to them. She had recognized in those cartoons many of the unanswered questions that had been raised in our sessions. She and I worked off those books for several months, using the author's expressive cartoons of his experiences with his father to guide us in discovering her family's silent vibrations.

Action: Move gently in exploring your parent's background, for internalized traumas are not always easy for people to share. You can add to your understanding by talking to people who experienced the same or similar traumas. Sometimes other members of the family are more open about the past and can more easily share the full impact of what had gone on. Getting them to share their stories expands and deepens the picture of what your parents' lives were like as children.

Look for other sources of information: books, films, articles, and lectures—even cartoons—that relate to the trauma. The more information you have, the more you will be able to understand how your parents may have been affected and thus to what kinds of vibrations you may have been reacting.

Point: For many years the question invariably asked was, "How does a child get the hidden messages of the inner world of the parent?" Neuroscience has begun to answer that question with the new understanding of implicit knowing and mirror neurons. As previously explained, implicit knowing—knowing how to be with others—is non-symbolic, non-verbal, and non-conscious, involving parts of the brain that do not require conscious processing during encoding or retrieval. It is generally associated with right brain communication and is present at birth. Mirror neurons, you will recall, explain the brain's reaction to the activity of another, without any action on the part of the viewer. It is a vital factor in such emotions and activities as empathy and imitation. It's doubtful if James ever heard his father speak of the concentration camp, or of the words of the elders, or of much else about his father's life. I believe that he did not. But James did experience his father's extreme isolation and distrust of others, and his father's fears and anxieties about how to exist in the world. James, like most children, was aware of and sensitive to experiences that were part of his life that should not have been, and others that should have been included but were not. For example, in the category of inappropriate inclusion was the father's insistence that James could play outdoors only if he, the father, was present. What were not included in James' life were people he could relate to, including his own mother. Underneath the father's overt behavior and language lay buried a layer of covert, subtle cues not visible to the eye—cues that, like the high-frequency whistles used to signal dogs, set up vibrations in the psyche of the child.

Action: Your imagination can be a valuable tool. For example, imagine your childhood as if it were a movie. Project it on a blank wall, sit back, and observe the action as if you were a member of the audience. Are there behaviors, people, or messages in the film that are incongruent to what would be the normal expected flow of action? The constant monitoring of James by his father would be seen as such an incongruity. And, conversely, are elements missing that would normally be part of the action? You may not be able to spot the entire dynamic; but each time you add a clue, you get closer to the reasons for your system.

Point: The same behavioral pattern can serve different environmental demands. For example, the adaptive behavior of James' need "not to speak" could meet other environmental demands, ones that are far less traumatic than James experienced. Important, too, is how a child interprets what appears to be a perceived demand. Remember, children think concretely and can misinterpret what is getting played out.

Sharing Betsy's history helps illustrate this point. Betsy, a young woman in her early twenties, had great difficulty in expressing herself and tended to be silent a good deal of the time. Her silence was making it more difficult for her to function in college.

Betsy poignantly recalled an incident that had occurred when she was in first grade. The class was singing Christmas songs and little Betsy was singing away. The music teacher quietly told a few of the children, Betsy among them, to "mouth the words, but don't make any sounds." Betsy remembered being hurt by this remark, particularly because she didn't know what she had done that was wrong. This incident became the model for her need to be silent, for Betsy's family maintained secrets that were not to be discussed outside the family. The child, not certain of what sounds she had made that were "wrong," became very cautious of making any sounds lest she unknowingly reveal the family secrets.

Once Betsy was able to uncover the connection between her family's secrets and the teacher's inappropriate comment, she began to allow herself more freedom in expressing herself. She discovered that one of the consequences of being silent for so long was her limited verbal vocabulary. Although she had an extensive understanding of the meaning of words and used them in her writing, she was unsure of how to pronounce them and so continued to remain intimidated by the fear of making the "wrong" sounds. She enrolled in a public speaking class, listened to vocabulary tapes, and told her friends to gently correct her mispronunciations.

Action: If you have been the "silent child," ask yourself what you can do to enhance your ability and comfort in learning how to speak freely. In exploring why you behave in ways that interfere with your reaching your potential, pay attention to any childhood experience that you may have misinterpreted, particularly if the incident fed into an environmental demand.

Point: Children will build some form of protection when the people in their world are experienced as intrusive, uncaring, smothering, or abusive. The barrier can be, like Len's, an internal one—a "glass" wall—that guards against invasion. The individual can see and be seen but not be touched or touch others.

There are other effective ways for children to defend their inner space. One is by turning off the sound. For example, Johnny's father yells at him whenever Johnny does anything wrong, calling him stupid, impossible, a pain in the butt, and so on. Johnny, hating the sound of those words, turns away. Father grabs him by the ears and forces a face-to-face confrontation while he continues his harangue. Johnny then turns off the dial that controls his hearing. He goes to school, hears the teacher say something, assumes another barrage of angry words, and again, turns off the sound. After awhile, as these episodes continue, Johnny loses control of the dial. As an adult, he is not able to fully control what he hears and may understand only 50 to 60 percent of any conversation. He may appear aloof or uninterested when, in reality, he is trapped in a pattern of unconscious censoring.

A third technique for protective survival entails deflection, which is also a result of verbal abuse. Based on past experience, Johnny automatically assumes he is the target of a verbal missile. Just before it reaches him, he deflects it by shifting the focus to someone or something else. The long-term effect of this system can result in Johnny alienating family and friends who complain that he is being "slippery," not taking responsibility, or hiding some negative deed.

Action: Take stock of how you relate to others and others relate to you. Check to see if you are caught in hidden barriers of protection. These barriers can vary and include: needing to remain apart from others; not trusting that others will respect your space; feeling threatened if another gets too close; having difficulty staying tuned in to conversations; having others complain that you are not available or interested in them; being seen by others as insincere, unreliable, or slippery; feeling trapped in a heavy schedule of work and/or activity. The recognition of a barrier is the first step toward breaking it down.

Point: Understanding how words are used—or misused—is essential. The following is a list of positive words or phrases that, when confused with negative ones, offer clues to survival systems. Clarifying their meaning has led many people to recognize their hidden barriers. Do you know the difference between:

- "involvement" and "intrusion"

- "deserving" and "indulging"

- "caring for oneself" and "being selfish"

- "successful" and "exploitive"

- "healthy ego" and "narcissistic"

- "responsibility" and "burden"

- "proud" and "vain"

- "shyness" and "snobbishness"

- "sensitive" and "weak"

- "neat" and "compulsive"

- "friendly" and "wanting something"

- "confident" and "egotistical"

- "assertive" and "aggressive"

- "to need" and "to be needy"

- "life is a process" and "life is a burden"

Action: Become aware of how you use language. It is helpful to check a dictionary for the actual meaning of words. Some words like "selfish" or "vain" are harsh and carry a punitive, judgmental connotation. Seeing the actual definition of a word can offer meaning as to what was "normal" in your world but not necessarily normal in a more universal world.

It is helpful to pay attention also to how others use or misuse words when referring to you or your actions. Are you called "selfish" when you appropriately meet your needs? How about "needy" whenever you ask for help? Is mother's behavior "dramatic" or "unstable"?

Point: The true power of a system can reside in the need of one parent to pacify the other parent, at the expense of the child. Len's system was particularly powerful because he got caught in his father's need to pacify his mother. His father's admonitions to "not upset your mother" forced Len to give in to the intrusive and smothering behavior of his mother. Any negative or oppositional reactions by Len would not only elicit a reaction from his mother, but also disapproval from his father. Len's need to not disappoint and alienate his father had strengthened his protective wall. This kind of situation often results in a child disappearing or becoming invisible.

Another vignette may help clarify this point. Carol disappeared into "unimportance." Although her children often called upon her for assistance, and friends would call her first if they needed help, she was convinced that she had little or no importance. Her belief in her unimportance had, over the years, dulled her life and hampered her attempts to feel joy and satisfaction. After all, whatever she did lacked importance, so why bother.

Carol, sensitive and somewhat anxious, came to understand that she had lived in a world where she had needed to be unimportant. Her mother was the "expert" on all things important and would advise, judge, and criticize the child. Any attempt to disagree with her mother or express her own opinion would lead to the admonishment by her father of "don't upset your mother." Carol was caught: if she stood up to her mother, she would anger and possibly lose her father, a loss she believed she would not survive. Her way out of this dilemma was to hide in "unimportance." As long as she believed that what she felt, believed, wanted, and wished for was unimportant, she was able to tolerate an intolerable situation.

Action: Evaluate your parent's relationship to see if you got caught between them. The fathers of both Len and Carol played the "protective" husband, forcing their children to passively accept the inappropriate behaviors of the mothers. The reverse can also be present when the mother, afraid of her husband's anger, cautions the children to not say or do anything that would upset him. Nor is this mother able to stand up to the father when he oversteps his parental authority.

In these cases, the survival system at first appears to be the result of the parent who was difficult, demanding, or dysfunctional. The other parent is often seen as the "good" one. But the real power of the child's survival system rests in the need of the child to satisfy the "good" parent's need for passive acceptance. Had Len's father not played the theme of "don't upset your mother," Len would not have been forced to swallow his mother's intrusions. I have also found that the "good" parent unknowingly causes a more painful wound in the child.

Remember, the child doesn't say, "My father has a need to not deal with my mother." The child feels, "If I were important enough, my father would stand up for me."

CHAPTER TWELVE

Family Secrets

Sometimes, the emergence of new symptoms, or the re-emergence of old ones, can signal the existence of a survival system.

The Need to Be Stupid: Diane

Diane had been in therapy before. She recently experienced several episodes of severe anxiety and decided to return for a second round. Her therapist, now retired, had referred her to me. "Something is wrong," she said, "I've struggled with a great deal in my life, but anxiety is new." Before we could explore what was going on, Diane wanted me to understand what she had discovered in her prior therapy. She began a monologue that stretched over several sessions. This is her story as she related it to me:

"I got into therapy because I fell apart. I started to cry one day and could not stop. My first child was a year old, life was good, and I had no reason to be so upset.

"The only recent event I could recall was my father-in-law's attempted suicide. My mother-in-law was unable to wake him one morning; and since we lived across the street, she called me and I ran over. I realized that he had taken an overdose of sleeping pills, and I called the police; the paramedics came and revived him. But that had happened over two months before, and I didn't believe it had affected me.

"Anyway, I started to see Dr. Rose. As we explored my childhood, it became apparent that I couldn't remember much of anything between the ages of six and twelve. Those were the years that my mother, father, and I shared a house in Brooklyn with my father's sister, her husband, and their two children.

"It's important that you know that my mother and father would not have won any prizes for parenting. My father traveled a great deal and my mother, in addition to working full time, was passionately involved in all kinds of causes. I later found out that the two families had decided to combine forces because my uncle was having financial problems and, with my aunt there to take care of me, my mother could have more freedom.

"When I was ten, my uncle died. I vaguely remembered that my mother, aunt, cousins, and I had gone to the movies one night and that all the lights were on when we got home. I also remembered my aunt and mother crying, neighbors running in, and my mother telling me that my uncle had died of a heart attack.

"Although Dr. Rose thought that the six-year gap in my memory was important, he believed it was more important to deal with my depression. We discovered enough reasons for it without delving into things I could not remember such as my parents not being available, particularly my mother, who chose her causes over me; the rotten feelings I had about myself because, after all, the starving children in whatever land were more important than I was; my dropping out of college and marrying at nineteen; my childhood fears; my shyness; my being a latch-key kid from the time I was twelve, and so on. Two years into my therapy, I was definitely better and had regained some of my lost memory. But I was not yet ready to stop therapy. And that's where it stood until a seemingly unrelated event occurred.

"Cynthia was my best friend in high school; and although we weren't good about keeping in touch, it was understood that we would always be friends. One day her husband unexpectedly called to let me know he was in town and, of course, I invited him to the house. He walked in escorting a woman I'd never met before. I waited for Cynthia, assuming she'd appear any moment. But when she didn't, I asked rather rudely where she was.

"He turned white and said, 'Don't you know?'

'Know what?'

'Cynthia died six months ago. Didn't anyone tell you? Your mother was at her funeral.'

'No, she never mentioned it.'

"I wrote a scathing letter to my mother about what she had done, what she should have done, and where she could go. A week later, I got a letter from her that blew me away. 'She was only trying to protect me,' she wrote, and hoped that one day I would forgive her. She swore that she would never keep secrets from me again. Then, unexpectedly, she told me the true story of my uncle's death.

"She confirmed that the five of us had gone to the movies, as I had remembered. Desperate to go to the bathroom when we got home, I had run ahead of everyone else. All the lights were on, as I had remembered, the front door was open and I had entered the house alone. I ran into the bathroom and must have seen that my uncle lay sprawled across the floor. According to my mother, he had hung himself from the shower curtain rod but the weight of his body had pulled the rod out of the wall and his body had dropped to the floor. He hadn't had a heart attack, he had killed himself, and I was the one who had found him.

"No wonder I had freaked out when my father-in-law attempted suicide.

"Three months later I finished my work with Dr. Rose. I never have been able to remember that awful night but somehow it doesn't matter. There is a part of me that's never forgiven my family for keeping that secret. Here I had experienced this terrible trauma and everyone had lied to me."

As Diane continued to tell me about her life since last seeing Dr. Rose, I became aware of how often she seemed to need reassurances that she was all right, in spite of her many accomplishments.

Life, she told me, had been good after her therapy. She had a second child and loved being a mother. Her marriage seemed stable, and she had reconciled with her parents. But then things began to change. She and her husband grew apart; and after several years, they decided to divorce. Being on her own set into motion a series of challenges that, as Diane met them, changed her greatly.

She returned to college and graduated with honors. "I chuckle," she said, "when I think of those college days. I was sure I was going to fail every exam. At first, my classmates were sympathetic; but after I kept on getting straight A's and pulling up the grading curve, they weren't too happy with me. It took me two more years of A's to believe that I wasn't going to fail."

She really did need reassurances, I thought. I began to suspect a hidden survival system.

After graduation, she secured a job in an advertising firm. Her immediate supervisor liked her, offered to train her, and within a year she had become an assistant to a midlevel account executive. The next year, she was promoted to assistant to one of the senior partners; and, recently, she had been made a junior account executive, responsible for several major clients.

I was impressed with her success in so short a time and told her so.

"Well," she said, "at least it proves that I'm not stupid." Her response was more self-denigrating than usual.

"Why stupid?" I asked.

"For a long time people didn't see me as being too sharp," she answered. "I was very quiet, didn't have much to say anyway, and I had difficulty talking because my words would get jumbled. I remember getting complimented, in the presence of my ex-husband, on how quickly I had learned to play chess. He started to talk about how he had loved playing the game. This was news to me, for I had never before heard him mention his interest in chess. I asked him why we had never played. 'Because I thought you were too stupid to learn,' he said. I guess I believed that too."

The discrepancy between the woman in these stories and the woman who sat facing me was striking. The Diane that I saw was attractive, articulate, and bright, a woman who had developed a successful career while mothering two children. The woman in her anecdotes believed she was unattractive, inarticulate, and stupid. And I knew that this "other woman" still existed in Diane because of the way she spoke about herself, consistently expressing genuine surprise at her own success and finding ways to put herself down.

Whenever I mentioned this discrepancy to Diane, she usually responded with some reference to the distortions surrounding her uncle's death. But I began to wonder if her uncle's death, although a major trauma, wasn't acting as a smoke screen. Perhaps there were more issues that were being kept secret and denied.

I began to press Diane for more details about the six missing years in her memory. She was able to recall anecdotes about her aunt and her two cousins but had few memories that included her father, mother, or uncle. I could understand her difficulty in recalling her father and her uncle, since one was tied to a trauma and the other was rarely home. But, I questioned, was her mother actually not part of the household or did she not remember her being there?

Diane's mother had held to her promise of not keeping secrets and had become a reliable source of information. Her mother was able to admit that she had kept busy pursuing her outside interests, assuming her child was being well taken care of by the aunt.

That kind of abandonment, I thought, could explain Diane's poor sense of self and lack of worth. But why stupid?

As Diane shared more memories, I began to perceive her childhood as being more difficult than she did. For example, she remembered that she had loved sweets and that one of her cousins would trick her by offering her goodies that were actually something else.

"Like what?" I asked.

"One time," Diane said with amusement, "she offered me a big piece of chocolate and it really was Ex-Lax. You can imagine what that did."

My response was that I would have been upset.

"Really," she said with surprise. "Everyone else thought it was funny."

It wasn't funny, I explained, because there was an element of meanness in her cousin's so-called "joke."

In many of Diane's stories she was the target of her cousins' cruel jokes and teasing. I commented that her cousins could not have been easy to live with. She agreed but replied that they didn't mean to hurt her.

As our sessions continued to uncover episodes that Diane believed funny and innocent, and I saw as mean-spirited and negatively competitive, her anxiety worsened. She began to experience panic attacks.

For someone who has never experienced a panic attack, it can be difficult to imagine how devastating a sensation it can be. The heart races, the body trembles, hyperventilation causes dizziness, and waves of fear and foreboding pound the body and psyche. Diane once described an attack as "feeling like I'm in the path of a hurricane and all I can do is hang on for dear life."

"Hang on to what?" I asked.

"My sanity," she replied.

It is not unusual for people to experience discomfort when they are subjected to probing questions, particularly questions that might reveal a system. But Diane's increasing anxiety seemed to indicate something else. She had no history of panic attacks, it was not a factor in her first therapy, and she had reported that she had not been an anxious child. I felt that I was overlooking some important information and went over once more what she had shared with me, trying to understand her history with new insight.

Somewhere in that process, I realized that the key, as is so often the case, was not in the information already known, but in what was missing. And so I asked Diane more probing questions:

"Why were your older cousins allowed to tease you to the point of harassment? Why was no one upset that you got a laxative instead of chocolate? We know that your mother and father weren't around, but where were your aunt and uncle when the teasing and 'jokes' were going on?"

Diane had no answers but took the questions to her mother. Her mother's difficulty in answering raised more questions. Like many secretive families, Diane's family needed to present itself as untroubled. Diane's steady questioning of her mother ultimately revealed what had existed under the seemingly smooth surface during the years the families had lived together.

Diane's father was home so seldom that his involvement was almost non-existent. Her mother had abdicated her parental responsibilities to the aunt and was only peripherally involved in the daily running of the household. The uncle was overwhelmed with a failing business and mounting debts.

"What about your aunt," I asked, "did you like her?"

"She was fine," Diane replied.

There was a tone in that answer that suggested there was more to be learned. Diane agreed to get more information from her mother, including how the mother felt about the aunt.

Her mother's answer was supportive of the aunt. But Diane had learned her lessons well and posed an interesting question. "I asked my mother if she knew how my aunt really felt about her. I knew by the look on her face that I had hit a nerve."

Her mother, with great hesitation, shared her belief that the aunt had not been happy. Diane's uncle had not been a good provider and had become, in the years before his death, depressed, withdrawn, and inclined to drink too much. Stuck with the children and household chores and living on limited means, Diane's aunt had become angry and resentful. Diane's mother admitted that she had indeed taken advantage of her sister-in-law and that her lack of involvement in family responsibilities had fueled the aunt's resentment. Since the adults in that family hid their feelings, not only from each other but from themselves as well, it was likely that some of those feelings were acted out among the children. And with Diane's mother unavailable, Diane became the primary target of the aunt's resentfulness.

I asked Diane what she thought about this new information. She was silent for a while and then said, "I always felt that my aunt didn't particularly care for me. She had a way of making me feel small, less important . . . I guess even stupid."

Diane gathered more information from others in her extended family until she had a better sense of the environment to which she had adapted. Tensions had brewed between the aunt and uncle as well as between the sisters-in-law, with a high level of unexpressed anger brewing among the adult family members. The manner in which the uncle had killed himself struck me as an extreme act of repressed rage.

Much of the new information explained why Diane thought (or needed to think) she was stupid. She realized that "being stupid" allowed her to be less of a target of the aunt's resentment. It also fulfilled her need to remain ignorant of the truth about her uncle's death as well as the crosscurrents of resentment that had swirled among the family members. It was not only reassurance she had sought from her straight A's, she had also been seeking permission to live up to her intellectual potential. But we still could not explain her anxiety attacks until she reported an incident at work.

An associate had expressed annoyance at the way Diane was treated by a senior partner at the last staff meeting.

"It was confusing," Diane said, "because I hadn't heard him say anything negative about me and didn't understand why she was offering sympathy."

I asked if her associate had given any details.

"Yes," replied Diane. "She said the partner was unfairly putting me down."

"Was he putting you down?" I asked.

"Well, he might have been a little upset. But if he said anything negative about me, I didn't hear it."

"Did the woman tell you what she thought she heard him say?"

"Not what he said, but her feeling was that he was making me the scapegoat for his mistake."

I could see that she was uncomfortable with this line of questioning.

I asked her if she knew if the partner had made a mistake.

"Well, it really wasn't a mistake," Diane replied, "it was more like a misunderstanding."

"Diane, it seems to me that you're denying something about this partner that echoes back to the way you used to deny the real meaning of your cousins' jokes." I caught a look of fear on her face and quickly asked, "What are you feeling, right at this moment?"

"I'm getting one of those horrible panic attacks." She started to cry.

I was able to calm her down and the session ended, knowing that we had touched something important.

I kept on playing the scene over and over again in my head, trying to spot—what? And once again I had to ask: What was missing? In particular, what was missing from Diane's reactions to being mistreated? Not words this time but feelings. What was missing was anger!

Most people would have had a reaction to the partner's demeaning behavior. Instead, Diane had started to have a panic attack when I confronted her. Does she have to substitute anxiety for anger, I asked myself? What had she said in an earlier meeting? "I feel like I'm in the path of a hurricane and can only hang on for dear life." There's no room for anger when one is hanging on for dear life.

I shared my thoughts with Diane at our next meeting and asked if there was a reason she would "need" not to feel anger.

She had no immediate answer except that her family, in general, had difficulty in dealing with anger. She did add that her most recent panic attack had followed that staff meeting.

Some time later, Diane mentioned that "she had this funny feeling that, maybe, she had had an argument with her uncle the night before he had killed himself." I took Diane's feelings seriously, for this could partially explain why she might be unable to feel anger, let alone express it.

"Children believe," I explained, "that they are the center of their worlds. As such, they also believe that they have powers to affect all things in that world. It is likely," I told her, "that you would have felt that your anger had caused your uncle's death. Your anger then becomes a dangerous weapon that must be controlled. What better way to control it than by not experiencing it."

After awhile, Diane was able to recognize that the partner had been harassing her and that the start of her anxiety attacks coincided with the start of his verbal attacks. Caught between her newfound emotional growth and her archaic need to be non-responsive, she had reacted internally by actively repressing her anger and converting it to anxiety.

She continued to struggle to overcome her anxiety but remained unable to hear when someone was putting her down. She started to make significant progress when she began to use her feelings of anxiety creatively, as a signal that she was being attacked. Her anxiety became a translator, for she was able to recognize that she was being put-down when her anxiety kicked up. She would then switch to another "channel"—hear what was really being said—and object to the comment.

Except for her continuing need to filter her anger through anxiety, she had more than met her original therapeutic goal. "But," she complained, "having to depend on anxiety as a

translator means I haven't gotten my system under control."
I counseled her to be patient and that control would come in
time.

One day Diane was telling me about a man she had recently
met. He had impressed her and seemed interested in her. I
decided to play devil's advocate in the hope that she would
be able to trust me enough to express anger at me. I started
to raise negative questions about him. As she tried to answer
my questions, her face reddened and her body stiffened. I
continued to press for more information about him until Diane
suddenly exploded.

"How dare you use that tone with me. I'm not a child and I
don't need to be treated like one. I . . ." She stopped. "Oh, my
God, I got angry! I actually got angry. No filters, no translators,
no channel switching—just pure, direct anger. Hallelujah!"

We both knew that this would be one of Diane's last sessions.

CHAPTER THIRTEEN

Family Myths

"**S**he's had a personality transplant," I said to myself, as Jackie walked out of my office that morning. The animated woman who laughed and joked as she shared amusing stories of her recent vacation on the Colorado River was not the same person I had been seeing for the last eight months. This Jackie exuded a sense of energy, light-heartedness, and enjoyment of life. The Jackie I knew was somber, serious, and burdened with responsibilities. Until that morning, I had assumed that her unhappiness was due to a combination of her poor self-image and the frustrations in her current life. Discovering what seemed to be a major discrepancy between the Jackie of today's session and the one I had come to know made me question my original assumption. Is it possible, I asked myself, that she's stuck in a survival system?

The Need to Be Responsible: Jackie

Let me first recount her background and the feel of our previous sessions. Jackie had originally sought therapy hoping to relieve the stress she had been experiencing at work. She felt caught in a situation that seemed to have no solution. On one hand, she had a high-paying job offering good medical benefits and a lucrative pension plan. On the other, her position had become more stressful, more demanding, and increasingly time-consuming. She did not want to leave a company where she had seniority and a twenty-year association. But she was afraid that she might be paying too high a personal price to stay. And yet, she felt she could not afford to give up the income and benefits the job offered. Our early sessions focused on this dilemma.

It had been obvious from the beginning of our sessions that her job was, in fact, demanding, that she had been covering for less effective employees, and that the company was probably taking advantage of her. But it was unfair to totally fault the company, for she did function as an especially competent staff member, able to handle complex issues. And she never refused an assignment. She might have reached her maximum capacity and been experiencing a minor meltdown. A woman who takes life very seriously, she probably was taking her job too seriously.

I had asked her what she imagined the consequences would be if she decided to quit.

"I don't think I could find another position that offers me the kind of money I'm now making. And I wouldn't, actually couldn't, take one for less," she had said.

My further questioning of her need for an equivalent salary revealed that she, as well as some other members of her family, was committed to helping her brother cover some of the losses he had sustained in various investments over the last few years. Although her husband earned a good living as a commercial pilot, he had resisted getting involved in his brother-in-law's problems. Jackie, feeling responsible, felt she had no choice but to help.

As our sessions continued, it had become more obvious that the weight of her job was only part of her stress, and we shifted our attention to her life away from work. Jackie and her husband had two grown children. She was solicitous toward her elderly parents and had a close bond with her sisters and brothers. Jackie took her responsibilities toward all of them even more seriously than she took those of her job.

I once had commented that it felt as if she were Atlas carrying the world on her shoulders.

"I did have a lot of responsibilities in my family," she had said. "After all, I was the eldest of four children and, as is usually the case, the eldest one is expected to help out."

As our sessions had continued, Jackie continued to play the "eldest one," helping out in ways that I had begun to question. For example, there was the incident of the Thanksgiving dinner. Her parents, who still lived in Oregon, where Jackie had been born, were vacationing in a desert resort about a three-hour drive from Jackie's current home. Her siblings, some of whom lived closer to where the parents were staying, thought it would be fun to have Thanksgiving dinner at the resort. In our session following that holiday, Jackie, had talked about the weekend and clearly did not appear to have had much fun. I had asked her about that.

"There's not much time to have fun when you're dealing with food for eighteen people," she had said. "Actually, I was quite clever in figuring out how to keep the turkey and all the trimmings hot so we wouldn't have to re-warm anything."

I commented that it sounded like she had once again found a solution to a difficult challenge and had probably cooked a good deal of the Thanksgiving dinner.

"Well actually," she had replied, "I brought all of it."

"But what about the others in the family? Didn't they help?"

"It was just easier for me to do it," she had answered.

I had begun to wonder if the problem lay in Jackie's inability to "Just say no!" She is a gentle and generous soul, of whom others tend to take advantage. I had shared these thoughts with her, and we had begun to focus on her learning how to determine when and how to establish better boundaries for herself. Her progress had been slow, but she had begun to improve. I had not seriously considered the possibility that she might be caught in a survival system until that morning when this new Jackie emerged, the Jackie of the personality transplant.

Now I looked forward to our next session, curious to see which Jackie would appear. I was ready to start asking: "Do you, for some unknown reason, have a need to not have fun?"

The Jackie of our next session was the serious one, burdened once again with responsibilities and commitments. I shared my belief that discrepancies are often the sign of a hidden survival system and suggested that we review her history again. This time a slightly different picture of her childhood emerged. Her earliest childhood memories were of being fussed over by her mother who had dressed her in fancy outfits and had patiently curled her blond hair into halos of ringlets. All that had changed with the birth of a brother when she was three and the subsequent birth of her twin sisters.

It is not unusual for the eldest child to assume some caretaking responsibilities for younger siblings. But the degree of her involvement in the family's functioning and the level of responsibility emerging from Jackie's new memories made me question whether there was more to her "seriousness" than having just gotten caught in the role of the eldest sister. And so we began to explore her family's dynamics from different angles, succeeding after awhile to open new doors.

"Did I ever tell you," Jackie said one day, "that my mother left me to take care of my younger brother when I was four years old and he was a year old?"

She hadn't mentioned that before and, at first, I was rather skeptical about the accuracy of her recollection. But a family member was able to confirm it. From that memory, as well as others, the emerging picture of her mother was of an immature woman who had little knowledge or awareness of what it meant to be a responsible parent. That surely could account for Jackie's overdeveloped sense of responsibility. But it didn't fully explain why there was such a discrepancy between the Jackie of the family and the Jackie of the vacation.

Sometimes there is an unexpected payoff in just wandering in an individual's life with no set questions in mind. I had casually asked Jackie what she was like in elementary school. As she shared various incidents relating to school, the laughing, animated Jackie appeared.

I was delighted to see her again. "You seemed to have been able to have fun in school," I commented. "It's almost as if school was a vacation."

"I was free in school," she answered. "I particularly loved it when we could go outside and play. When I didn't have to worry about the phone ringing or one of the kids crying or an unexpected delivery."

"Why would you have had to worry about ringing phones or crying kids?" I asked. "I had to be able to tell my mother what was going on," she answered.

"All right," I asked, "why would you have had to be able to tell your mother that, say, the phone was ringing? Couldn't she hear it?"

"No," she answered. "That was the problem. My mother was deaf, but we all pretended that she wasn't. The family knew, of course. The neighbors probably knew or at least thought that she was hard of hearing. Actually, anyone who had any consistent dealing with her must have known that she couldn't hear. But Mom acted as if she could. For example, we would go into a store and she would ask the clerk a question. The clerk would answer and Mother would knowingly nod her head. Then, as soon as we would leave, she would immediately ask me what the clerk had said. That went on all the time."

That was another moment when I could only shake my head in awe of the power of family myths to bury important facts. I asked Jackie why she had never mentioned this before.

"I guess I never thought to mention it," she said. "It wasn't a secret. I believe a number of people knew about it and accepted it. And accepted Mother's pretending to hear. It was just one of those things that was!"

As Jackie continued to share "what was," the reasons for her seriousness became even more obvious. It appeared likely that most people actually did not know about her mother's deafness, and those who did gave little thought to the effects of "the myth of mother's hearing" on the children, particularly Jackie.

I asked about her father's role in maintaining the illusion of mother's ability to hear. And from her recollections it was clear that her father was as much invested in the myth as her mother. With father a participant in the charade, family life was slightly skewed. For example, Jackie remembered dinners as a time when mother would talk to one child at a time. She would look directly at that child, ask a question, and the child was expected to answer clearly and slowly, enunciating each word. There was no general conversation among the children or the father because "mother didn't like to be left out." Family time together was cumbersome, stressful, and often a burden.

Her parents' need to maintain the myth, reinforced by her mother's immaturity, had effectively acted to deny Jackie her childhood. Beginning with the birth of her brother when she was three, Jackie had to be available to hear a crying child or a phone ringing or a neighbor knocking on the door. While Jackie was in school, mother had a hired helper. But the woman was only part-time and that meant that Jackie was expected to go home immediately after school and either stay there or accompany her mother on any chores outside of the house.

"I was not allowed to play outside as long as my responsibilities required me to be available to my mother," she said.

"And you've been caught in that 'house of responsibilities' ever since," I said. "No wonder it feels like you're carrying the cares of the world on your shoulders. Do you realize what an enormous burden you carried as a child?"

Jackie was silent. And then she began to share some of her painful memories. "I used to sit by the window and watch my friends playing in a nearby park. I could hear them laughing and having fun. I wanted more than anything to be able to run outside and join them. But I knew that I couldn't. That it wouldn't be fair to my mother and the younger children. And that my father would be very upset."

I asked her if she recognizes the "echoes" of her childhood in her current struggles. "We can get major clues—those clues that we are always looking for in trying to understand our survival systems—from our adult issues. Are you not playing a similar role in your job?"

Jackie's recognition of those "echoes" was the beginning of her learning how to give herself permission to refuse inappropriate and unnecessary responsibilities at work. Her supervisors and co-workers were, at first, surprised and annoyed by her newfound independence. But Jackie was too valuable a player to be unduly criticized, and most of the staff recognized that she had been carrying more than her share.

One day I asked her to imagine how, as a child, she might have experienced her world.

"Let's see," she answered, "children think concretely and assume that, if anything is wrong, it must be because of them. I imagine that I must have believed that I was less valuable than my siblings and could, and probably should, be stuck in the role of my mother's 'ears.' That I must have done something or not been something that justified my not being allowed to play. That my real value was in my being responsible—and not in just being me. And since 'me' wanted to play, my playing wasn't important. That I internalized that belief and it generalized to include everything I did." She paused and then said, "Did I get it right?"

She got it right! And understood, for the first time, why she had never felt good about herself. Why, except for vacations away from home, she had never allowed herself to relax and enjoy leisure time.

Life was definitely improving for Jackie, and she was well on her way to having her life be less burdensome. It seemed an appropriate time for her to stop therapy, with the understanding that she was free to return should she require more help in the future.

Eighteen months later, Jackie was back. The company was offering a few employees the opportunity of taking early retirement, and Jackie was among those chosen. She believed that it was a legitimate offer, wanted to take advantage of it, but was concerned and uncertain about losing her steady income. Although her work situation had greatly improved, she had continued to feel that her job was demanding and draining much of her energy. And having discovered, in our earlier sessions, her sense of the loss of her childhood and her deep longing for play, she had increasingly wanted to drastically change her lifestyle.

I asked her why she believed she couldn't leave the company. Since her husband was able to support them both, why not find something more appropriate to her present needs or possibly not work at all.

And once more she brought up the issues surrounding her not being able to give up her present income. As we talked, it became even more evident that the reasons for that income were tied to a need to be supportive of her brother by helping to cover his debts. I questioned whether her feeling that she had no choice was, in any way, another "echo."

"It doesn't sound like you *want* to help him," I said, "but rather *need* to help him. Is it a 'Snow White' need?"

At first, Jackie could make no connection. But as we touched on the myth of her mother's hearing, she became very silent. There was a long pause and then slowly, very slowly she said, "I think my family has another myth going. My brother has replaced mother as the one needing to be wrapped in a myth. There's been this pretending that he's an investment genius and that, one day, he'll make a killing in the market or real estate that will make him a fortune. This supposed new real estate deal that he was going to buy into—there's always a great new deal on the horizon—is just one more example of how he gets the family, particularly me, to commit to help cover any losses. And, of course, I fell right into it."

And Jackie was right! Her brother, who worked in an accounting firm, had begun years ago, to see himself as experienced and competent in investment strategies. He would talk about all sorts of investments for making big money while consistently losing more than he made. Invariably the family would help cover his losses. Jackie had no idea of how much money she had contributed, but she was finally able to recognize that she had been the family member expected to give the most financial support and that she had been sacrificing her freedom in order to maintain her brother's illusions. Her husband, who had washed his hands of the whole business, had remained silent about the matter.

I asked her how she felt about his lack of support.

It took awhile, but Jackie was again able to recognize another "echo."

"I imagine," she said, "that I interpreted his silence in the same way I did the silence of the adults in my childhood. And that silence validated my mother's inappropriate behavior."

And again she was right.

I agreed that it meant that, once again, she was on her own with no choice but to play her usual supportive part.

Jackie returned to our next session determined to break the hold of family myths and to make some important changes in her life. "I'm going to take my early retirement," she said. "I'm sure my family will be extremely upset with me, but I'll be able to handle that. I have wanted to be free all of my life; and I know that if I don't start enjoying life and having some fun now, I never will."

And again, Jackie was right. She recently sent me a picture of herself standing in her full-flowered garden, bathed in bright sunlight.

CHAPTER FOURTEEN

Family Power

To be honest, I was not looking forward to seeing Emily this day. Although we had established a good working relationship, the past six months had been particularly difficult for both of us. She had continued to remain stuck in ambivalence about her marriage, and I was struggling with an ethical dilemma. Unless she could hold to a decision about whether to stay or leave her marriage, she could not move forward with her life. And I was beginning to feel that she was wasting her money by continuing in therapy with me. The question of when is it appropriate to encourage a patient to continue to work with me versus when is it necessary to recognize that doing so is not in the best interest of that individual, is never an easy one to answer. I had decided, after our last session, that it was time for us to discuss ending her therapy with me. She might do better with another therapist or possibly another kind of therapy.

The Need to Not Decide: Emily

Sitting in my office that morning, I had time to review our work together one more time to make sure I had reached the appropriate conclusion. I carefully checked off the salient points of information I had gathered.

Emily had started therapy because she was concerned about her marriage and confused about her feelings toward her husband. At the time of her first visit, she had been married for thirteen years. Although now questioning whether she wanted to remain in her marriage, it was clear that the early years had been positive. They both had well-paying positions that allowed them to afford the home they purchased several years after their wedding. And both agreed that having children could wait.

"I adored him," I remembered her saying. "In those early years, John seemed to be all I had ever wanted."

I had asked what had changed.

She responded in her typical vague style. "I began to question whether we were compatible. Whether we wanted the same out of life."

"What do you want out of life?" I had asked. "What do you think you want out of this marriage?"

My early attempts to get her to articulate what she hoped to achieve generally failed, nor was I able to reach a fuller understanding of what had gone wrong in her marriage.

"We still have a good time when we do things together," she would say. "But those times seem to get less and less frequent. I think it's more a question of attrition than any specific problem or event."

Attempting to clarify her feelings, she had begun making lists: General assets and liabilities of her marriage, his good points and bad ones, what she could live with and what was unacceptable, what could change and what could not, what she must have in her life and what she could live without. The lists didn't help.

Over the months, a clear pattern had emerged. Emily would move toward staying in her marriage. A conflict would flare between her and her husband and she would move toward leaving. John would do something she experienced as caring and she would move toward staying. She would go out of her way to please him, he would unfairly criticize her, and she would move toward leaving.

We have not been able to make much of a dent in that pattern, I thought, as I waited for her. That's what is so frustrating. We still don't have a clear idea of what purpose, if any, the pattern serves.

I began to review her family history. Her father had been in the military for most of his life. Emily, her mother, and younger sister had followed him as he moved from one assignment to another. According to Emily, the family was run along military lines, with father being the general and the children new recruits. I'm not sure what military position mother held. The family moved every two or three years, resulting in Emily attending four elementary schools.

Over time it had become more obvious that Emily's current struggles had their roots in her past. The frequent moves would have made her more dependent on her family for continuity and support. And although Emily was able to establish new friendships as she moved from one state to another, one army base to another, one school to another, she felt that she had missed what others take for granted.

Answering my question of what she thought she had missed, she had said, "I guess a sense of having a real home. You know, a place that just belongs to you, that you can come back to year after year—where everybody knows your name."

The meaning of her longing for a place of her own only became understandable much later.

And what about loyalty, I said to myself that morning as I waited to see her. That's another of Emily's issues. Both of her parents were politically conservative and strongly supportive of this country's military involvement in Vietnam. Emily, then a young adolescent, had become emotionally responsive to the anti-war movement.

"I know they've never forgiven me," she had said. "As far as they were concerned, I was a terrible person, an ungrateful daughter, a turncoat—a traitor of the worst kind. They not only blasted me for being against the war, they could not believe that I could or would hold any ideas that were so disloyal to my country. They still have a fit any time there's a mention of that time."

I asked her if her difficulty in deciding what to do with her marriage also touched on questions of loyalty.

"Probably," she said. "Loyalty was very important in my family."

Emily's dream, as a young girl, had been to develop her artistic talent and become a professional artist, a dream encouraged by various teachers and friends. Her parents believed she was making a serious mistake and urged her to choose a profession that offered security. So Emily enrolled in college, planning to complete an advanced degree that would enable her to find a secure teaching position.

She discovered that she had a talent for languages and enrolled in a program offering several languages. While working on her bachelor's degree, she became a student of a professor of German who saw her as a promising disciple. Through a process that still eludes her understanding, Emily enrolled in a doctoral program with a major in German. She left the program when she married.

It didn't take much insight to know that Emily hadn't been happy about her choice of a major. And one day I had asked her what language she would have preferred to study.

"French," she had answered. "I would have been happier with French."

And *French* became our password for the discrepancy between what she would have wanted and what she invariably chose. According to her, French was light, airy, artistic, and sexy. German was heavier and tied to security.

With few exceptions, Emily never seems to do what Emily wants, I thought, as I reviewed her history. It's been a consistent theme from the beginning. And a theme we have been unable to understand fully and change, no matter how many times I'd ask, "Do you, for some unknown reason, have a need to not do what you want?"

But at least she had been able to make changes in her professional life.

When I first met her, she had a position as a specialist in development in a prestigious think tank. Emily felt that there were a number of positives to her job, including her seniority and the security the job offered. But she felt she was not being challenged and that the job had become routine and repetitive.

"Am I dealing with French and German again?" she had asked.

"What do you think?" I had answered.

"It's German!" she said.

She began to recognize how she was playing out a familiar pattern of ambivalence with her primary supervisor. She experienced her supervisor as demanding and often unappreciative of her efforts. Periodically she would move toward leaving her job. Her supervisor would soften his demands and she would move toward staying. Occasionally, when the vibrations were particularly bad, she would interview for another job but not get an offer. She was convinced that she had no choice but to stay and make the best of it. And I became convinced that she was sabotaging her interviews.

Emily began to realize that she might unknowingly be undermining her attempts to find a new position and approached the process differently. She found a new agency; and we worked on her interviewing skills, checking to see if she was sending any messages of disinterest. After several attempts, she was able to secure a position more to her liking, offering more challenges, money, and benefits.

Yes, she had been able to change, I thought. I went back in my mind to her history. Her parents had divorced a few years before Emily's marriage, with her father subsequently remarrying and moving to another state. Emily felt that he still tended to play "the general," occasionally making remarks that would make her feel like a raw recruit as well as a "bad" daughter. And she remembered how, as a child, she would hide her anger when he demanded total obedience in his harsh military style. Her mother would usually intercede, assuring Emily that her father loved her and was only doing what he believed was best for her. As she had begun to assert herself lately, regarding minor family matters such as visits and gifts, her father's critical comments had increased. She also had been upset with her father when he tried to involve himself in questions of her marriage. But overall, his effect on her current life seemed minimal.

In her earlier sessions, Emily had struggled to establish a more equitable relationship with her mother who was, at least to all appearances, the more influential parent. But she had been—and still was—far too involved in Emily's life. Over time Emily had been successful in establishing new boundaries between them. And although there would be conflicts between what Emily wanted and what her mother wanted, these differences did not have enough power to fuel her entrenched system.

As I sat there reviewing the details of her therapy, I kept coming back to her pattern of indecision, particularly as it related to her marriage. The changes she had made over these years were good, but not good enough to free her from her inability to decide what she wanted to do about her marriage. Of course, I thought, as long as she remains undecided, she can't move forward and get what she wants. And there is that "need to not get what she wants" again.

Then I remembered the issue about the house. She had fallen in love with a house that she and her husband had purchased. And the house had a garden that became an outlet for her creative talents. It was the home of her childhood dreams, the home that was the symbol of stability and continuity. After several years, her husband began to feel the house was an unnecessary financial burden and had begun to talk about selling it in order to take advantage of a good market. It seemed to me that John had his own issues regarding his value in his world and possibly felt that he was now less important to Emily than the house—that he was saying, "If you loved me you would be willing to give up the house." As I began to understand the dynamics of their relationship, it was his denial and resentment of the importance of the house to Emily, as well as her reaction to his reaction that fueled the growing schism between them. I remembered explaining to Emily my metaphor of how to understand the power of reactions.

I had once seen a film that tried to explain what happens in a nuclear reaction. The filmmakers had filled a small room with mousetraps, each holding a ping-pong ball. All was quiet. Then a single ping-pong ball was tossed into the room—the one and only action. After that action, what occurred was all reaction, with mousetraps springing their balls in response to being hit. In just a few seconds the room exploded in a blizzard of ping-pong balls.

As I explained to Emily, any one of us can have an unresolved issue that sits inside our psyche, not unlike a mousetrap holding a ping-pong ball. When someone we are close to also has a mousetrap, it takes only one action to set off an explosion. One of us says something that causes a reaction in the other. The other reacts and says something in reaction. The other reacts to the latest reaction, thus setting off a new round of reactions until, in a few seconds, there's an explosion.

I had asked Emily what she thought her "mousetrap" might be holding.

She was silent for a time and then said, "A lack of appreciation for who and what I am."

Emily's ambivalence about her marriage had continued, with John finally forcing a change. He had felt that he needed to move on and had unexpectedly accepted a position requiring him to immediately move to another region of the country. Now Emily struggled with whether she should follow him or stay in Los Angeles. Since John was opposed to a bicoastal arrangement, her staying would end their marriage. Her going, on the other hand, would end her way of life here and would include having to sell the house she loved. For the last six months she had been going back and forth—does she go or does she stay; and if she goes, what happens if it's not right?

Each week she would leave my office with some idea of what she wanted to do and return the next week to begin the questioning again. She seemed to be tilting in the direction of ending her marriage, but she was incapable of actually making the decision. She then tried to come to some mutual understanding with John about their differences should she decide to join him, but he was adamant that he could not make any promises. And that is where the matter stood that morning as I waited for Emily to arrive, unchanged in my belief that a decision must be made regarding her therapy.

Emily arrived and began to tell a story that allowed us to solve the mystery of her ambivalence. In essence, this is what she related:

"My mother came to see me yesterday with a confession. Seems that she had been speaking to my dad a month or so ago, and he told her that he was planning to write me a letter expressing his dissatisfaction with what I was doing with my life. She asked him to send her a copy. She received a copy of my father's letter, was upset about its content, and rushed over to my house to get the letter before I saw it. It turns out I was home that day, and I remember wondering why she had appeared and then disappeared so abruptly. Anyway, she managed to take the letter from the mailbox. Then she realized that my father would probably be even more upset when I didn't acknowledge his letter. So she decided to confess and gave me the three-page, single-spaced, typed letter. I don't know what to make of it. Whether to laugh or cry. What do you think of it?"

And she handed me her father's letter. It would have been amusing if it didn't personify the struggle Emily had been caught in for so many years. In essence, her father made it clear that she was not old enough, mature enough, wise enough, and strong enough to be able to make her own decisions—that her unwillingness to consult him on all things large and small was what was ruining her life. His comment about her therapy was typical: "How can your therapist help you when she has not spoken to me?"

Emily saw the look on my face and knew what I was thinking. "I guess as far as my father is concerned," she said, "I'm still a young, green recruit needing to follow orders. And recruits are only supposed to say 'Yes, sir.' Is that why I can't make a decision or be able to fully commit to it?"

"I don't think so," I answered. "It seems to me that the core of your system didn't spring from your not being able to decide. Neither was it a need to not get what you want. I think it was a need to not know what you want. For as long as you don't know what you want, power rests in the other person."

"But," Emily asked, "why didn't I see how my father's power was still trapping me in not being able to decide things for myself?"

"Recognizing his need to be in charge would have lessened his power," I replied. "The need not to see inappropriate parental needs is part of the function of a survival system. Remember, Snow White needed to see the stepmother as the fairest of them all."

This time Emily had no difficulty in recognizing her mother's actions as intrusive. They reminded Emily of an earlier pattern of mother interpreting father's actions, making excuses for him or, as in this case, interceding to avoid having to make excuses. In any case, both parents had sent, and were continuing to send, strong messages that Emily could not survive without them.

Emily's recent objections to some of her father's comments and intrusions had evidently stirred the pot, to the point where he felt he had to make a stand. As for her mother, she was finally able to recognize the inappropriateness of her intrusive protectiveness. Emily was also able to reinterpret the meaning of her parents' reaction to her anti-war sentiments. It was not her loyalty that had been in question. Their unforgiving, judgmental reactions were because she dared to hold ideas and beliefs that were different from theirs.

"I think I'm beginning to sense what might have happened between John and myself," Emily said. "The house was the first thing that I knew I truly wanted. And I wonder if, having the experience of knowing what I wanted, getting it, and holding on to it allowed me to recognize that there were other things I wanted. I can see how John could have been threatened by that, particularly if he needed to remain the most important thing in my life."

Emily's father could not have imagined how his letter freed her. She recently pursued and accepted a challenging new position, offering her enough money to enable her to keep the house—and remain in Los Angeles.

CHAPTER FIFTEEN

Changing the Effects of Secrets, Myths, and Power

POINTS TO MAKE
ACTIONS TO TAKE

Point: An individual can suffer from the direct effects of a childhood trauma and also be caught in a survival system in response to needing to avoid a second, more hidden trauma. Diane first sought help because of her depression. That therapy focused on her parents' unavailability, her shyness, insecurity, and sense of unimportance, all of which had been contributing factors in her depression. Her emotional reaction to her father-in-law's attempted suicide was symptomatic of the severe trauma she had suffered when she had found her uncle dead. Using the metaphor of the Snow White stories, this therapy would be similar to that required in a Tale of Reaction—a Snow White who experienced the overt traumas of her childhood.

Diane's second round of therapy uncovered her adaptive survival system, comparable to that of Snow White from a Tale of Survival. In the fairy tale, the destructive force that required a survival adaptation was the stepmother's envy. In Diane's case, the destructive force was the resentment of her aunt, played out as "teasing" and "jokes" by her cousins. Her aunt could have a sense of power and retribution by having her children best her rival's child. It was as if the aunt would look in the magic mirror and ask: "Whose children are the smartest of them all?" And the answer had better not be Diane.

Being "stupid" kept Diane's intellectual potential at a less dangerous level, for developing her full potential would have made her even more vulnerable to her aunt's resentments. It would be like the snowshoe hare *not* turning white in winter.

Action: Don't assume that you took either a "direct hit" from your environment or that you "ducked" its dangers. A child is vulnerable to both when adults in a family have psychological problems, unresolved issues, addictions, are particularly immature, have suffered their own childhoods, and are therefore not able to protect their children from the effects of adult dysfunction. When an individual seeks help, most often it is his or her overt reaction to a dysfunctional environment that becomes the focus of the healing process. Trauma reactions and the history of a trauma or a difficult childhood tend to be closer to the surface. But, as Diane found, a complex, hidden survival system can exist beneath the surface as a *childhood adaptation to a different danger in the same environment.*

Point: Family histories that demand secrecy are, by definition, damaging environments. Diane's second environmental demand required that she not reveal the secret of her uncle's suicide or the hidden negative feelings among the adults. Her experience of "being stupid" thus reinforced her maintaining the family secrets.

Secrets, such as a mother's psychiatric hospitalization, a father's imprisonment, a grandmother's drinking problem, being conceived before Mom and Dad got married, Mom and Dad never getting married, create a conspiracy of silence. Sometimes the child knows the secret, sometimes not. In either case, the secret is attached to a negative and/or punitive belief system that sends a signal that something or someone is "bad."

One of the results of maintaining such secrets is the sense of shame that is often the underlying reason for the existence of secrets in the first place. Shame relates to feelings of inadequacy and self-contempt by an individual, a family, or a group. To be ashamed is to assume rejection or derision, not because of what one has done but because of what one is or is not. Shame is less about morality and more about character, conformity, and how you are seen and accepted by others.

Secrets that are particularly powerful are ones that create fear and stress associated with the consequences of the secret being revealed. Imagine being a child who knows the secret of Dad's illegal dealings and fears that any hint of it could send him to prison. At school, when a teacher asks questions about your home life, you minimize the answers. When others talk about what their fathers do, you remain silent. When asked to speak in class, fearing giving the secret away, you start to stammer.

One of the results of getting caught in the fear of revealing a dangerous family secret is turning into a "silent child." A consequence of this is a limited ability to pronounce words correctly based on a lack of practice, which in turn increases your need to remain silent. This internal restriction on your "free speech" can result in limiting your academic and/or professional advancement as well as your spontaneity.

Another destructive consequence of family secrets is the effect they have on the child's sense of reality, particularly when the child senses but cannot confirm a secret. A discrepancy develops between what the adults say is reality and what the child senses is another, more negative and dangerous reality. This discrepancy is a breeding ground for unspecified anxiety in a child.

And still another impact of family secrets is the eroding effect they have on a child's ability to trust adults. If the child knows the secret, she comes to believe that adults don't tell the full truth. And if the secret is hidden, discovering it can lead to a sense of betrayal. As Diane said, "There is a part of me that's never forgiven my family for keeping that secret (her uncle's death). Here I had experienced this terrible trauma and everyone had lied to me."

Action: To break the negative hold of long-buried secrets, share them with close friends. Exposing secrets lessens their power and takes them out of the realm of being "unspeakable." It's like turning the lights on and discovering that the scary figure in the corner is a stuffed animal and not some creature that will destroy you.

Ask yourself if you have ignored "vibrations" in your family that might be covering unspoken secrets. Are there unexplained gaps and subtle distortions in the way your family history is told? Questions family members seem to ignore or avoid answering? Discrepancies between the reality the family maintains existed and what you, as an adult, would recognize as being impossible?

If you are still struggling with the effects of being a silent child, take classes to expand your ability to speak more freely and effectively. Ask friends to help you pronounce certain words, instead of making fun of your struggle to get them right. Check with others as to whether they see you as too formal, withdrawn, overly protective of your privacy, or lacking spontaneity.

Point: Seemingly dysfunctional behavior can act as a clue to a hidden system, as well as an effective tool to counteract that system. Diane's anxiety attacks before and during her therapy were *secondary adaptive responses* protecting her from experiencing and expressing her anger. Diane's recognition that her anxiety was a signal that she was being exposed to a negative interaction offered her a method of dismantling her system. Let's review that process. Diane's survival system did not allow her to hear or recognize when another person was demeaning or unfairly critical of her. Her emotional growth had changed that, but now her internal response to a negative comment elicited a reaction of anxiety. Why anxiety? Because there is no room for anger when one is being bombarded with anxiety. Diane began to use this reaction as a signal that she was being, as she called it, "zapped." Over time, she was able to quickly respond to that anxiety cue even as the other person continued to talk. Diane could then object to the comment as if she had heard it directly.

Action: Start by becoming sensitive to your emotional, verbal, and physical reactions to people or situations. Examples of such reactions include: feelings of anxiety, feeling overwhelmed, feeling small and insignificant, stammering, not being able to think or speak coherently, sudden rapid and/or breathless speech, unexpected yawning, sleepiness, or a drop in energy. Use the new awareness of your reaction as a signal that you may be reacting to someone or something triggering your survival system. As Diane discovered, the faster the time between the awareness of your reaction and your recognition of what is happening in your environment, the more power you will have to change the environment.

Point: The environmental demand to avoid a competitive situation can be played out in many ways. Snow White, needing to be "ugly," represents a survival system in response to the narcissism of a family member. Diane's need to be "stupid" was an adaptation enabling her to duck the danger from her aunt's competitive battle against Diane's mother. Quite different from Diane's system is a man who seems to "love having fun" and who doesn't want to get caught in the "trap of materialism." His may be a system of "not taking life too seriously." But his behavior may be meeting a hidden demand that he not be more successful than his father, for a father who destructively competes with his young son sends a message that the son had better not win the competition. The first-born child in a family, feeling insecure and no longer special with the arrival of the new baby, can play out those feelings by having to consistently best the younger child. The younger child, in turn, adapts by developing behaviors that guarantee mediocrity or failure. Cousins can get caught in acting out competitions among themselves that are the echoes of the competitions among the adults in the family. And adults in a family can get caught in competitions that are the echoes of previous generations.

One of my favorite stories is of "Aunt Bell and her chocolate cake." Aunt Bell was known for her wonderful chocolate cake and was very generous in sharing her recipe. The young women in the family would invariably ask her for the recipe and she would always freely offer it—but somehow it never was quite right. One day the cousins got together and started comparing the chocolate cake recipe that Aunt Bell had given each of them—and discovered that no two were the same. She had changed one or two ingredients in each recipe just enough so that no one's cake could ever be as good as hers, nor could the original recipe be known.

Action: Recognize the difference between competition that emphasizes sportsmanship, fairness and respect, and that which sends the message that winning is all—in any way you can and at any cost to another. Excessive teasing, "innocent" jokes, cutting remarks, lying to gain an advantage, can be signals of destructive competition. Check your family dynamics for obvious as well as hidden competitiveness between and among the adults and between and among the children. Ask yourself if you had permission to win, or were you the designated "loser."

Also check to see if family members put each other in no-win situations. For example, your family has a history of competitiveness among its members and you, being the youngest, are always destined to fail. Your two older brothers— who have had a falling out—have each invited you to their holiday dinner. What do you do? Clearly this is a lose/lose situation, for whichever invitation you accept, the other brother will be hurt, disappointed, or angry; and you will continue to feel like you've somehow failed. You make a list of what you lose if you go to brother A and what you lose if you go to brother B. Your decision is then based on which is the lesser of the two losses. A third choice, possibly offering the least loss, may be to find a reason for an unexpected trip out of town.

Point: When trying to break through to potential, it is important to recognize that an individual can be struggling with both having taken a "hit" and getting caught in a pattern of "ducking." A mistaken assumption is that the behavior and/or emotional state associated with each would necessarily be different. In Diane's case they were different: depression as a result of her dysfunctional environment and anxiety as a protection against her being able to express her anger at the way she was being—and had been—treated. In some cases, however, the behavior or emotional reaction may be exactly the same but tied to both reaction and adaptation.

Hank is an example of such a case. Hank existed in chronic confusion and sought help in gaining better control over his life, a life that was stuck in indecision. He struggled trying to decide what profession he wanted to pursue, which graduate schools would be best, what scholarships would be available, did he need a new car, would the old car last, and so on.

At first, his history offered a reasonable explanation for his confusion. Hank was the second of four children; and when he was nine, his mother suddenly died. The cause of her death was never discussed, leaving the children confused as to what had really happened. A year later, his father married a woman who had three young children of her own. Hank recalled a household of chaos and uncertainty.

Hank worked on establishing order in his life and was able to make some changes. But real change eluded him. He made lists of the positive and negative results of possible decisions and would lose the lists. He asked others for their opinions and was unable to recall what they said. He would spend hours researching something that required a decision but stop short of a solution. He stayed stuck in confusion.

Hank then shifted his focus and began to ask, "Do I need to be confused?" Turning his behavior into a possible survival system, he was finally able to answer his question. His father had needed that there be one, and only one, authority in the family. Consequently, any decision made without father's involvement and approval would be judged wrong. Hank was caught in a classic "no-win" situation. If he allowed his father to make decisions, he would feel negative about himself and resentful of his father. If he made decisions for himself, he would be attacked and told he was wrong and not smart enough to make the right choice. He solved the dilemma by staying in a state of confusion, for as long as he was confused, he could not make a decision.

Action: Recognize that there are no set patterns of reactions to guide you in uncovering both the traumas and adaptations of your childhood. Each child will respond to a dysfunctional environment in keeping with his or her own uniqueness, and each will adapt in ways that are consistent with his or her temperament and emotionality. Your approach to solving why you are not the person you want to be or not successful at getting what you want to achieve requires that you avoid getting caught in early assumptions about behavior, emotions, or yourself.

Point: Although the difference between a family myth and a family secret is not always clear, there is an important difference. That difference requires different paths to the understanding and unraveling of the subsequent systems. Let's use an image of an elephant to make the point.

The Secret: The family has hidden an elephant in the basement and no one is supposed to know about it. If word got out, the family believes that they would be shunned, the neighbors would be shocked, and life would never be the same. The elephant in the basement is the family secret.

The Myth: Now imagine that the family has an elephant in the parlor. Everybody in the family knows about it and some of the neighbors are semi-aware. The family members go about their business as if the elephant was the family cat.

Her mother's deafness wasn't a secret, it "just was." That is why it never occurred to Jackie to recognize it as an important "demand" in her childhood environment. The very nature of secrets and the vibrations surrounding them make them easier to spot. But myths, because they become woven into the fabric of the child's life, tend to be accepted as real and thus overlooked.

Action: One of the reasons a family establishes a myth is to deflect some characteristic of a family member that the individual member, in collusion with the family, experiences as dysfunctional or defective and therefore unacknowledgable. This perceived negative characteristic is then denied by being wrapped in a myth of non-existence. In Jackie's case, it was the mother's loss of hearing. In another case, it was the alcoholism of the father. There the myth was that father worked hard, was stressed, and needed help in relaxing—and could stop drinking anytime he chose. And a myth in another family was that mother was an adorable "Auntie Mame" character who was so amusing. The truth was that mother was not always functional and did not always recognize reality. Like the elephant in the parlor, the family and close friends chose to portray her as a "funny" lady, ignoring the potential danger to the children.

Point: The "me" of a survival system can be different from the "me" of one's innate potential. For example, the impression most people had of Jackie was that she was a person who took life very seriously, was somber and dour, and had little time or inclination for having fun. She seemed to welcome responsibilities, her own as well as others, and had a surrounding aura of chronic seriousness. The Jackie of vacations was quite different—laughing, light-hearted, and energetic. Only her husband, children, and the people with whom she might be sharing the vacation would know this Jackie. It was the Jackie I discovered in the session following her vacation and limited for some time to only that one session.

Action: Ask yourself if there is a different "me" waiting to be free. Do others only see the "you" of your survival system, while you sense that there is something in you still untapped? The image to keep in mind is that of a butterfly unable to emerge from a cocoon and having everyone assume it is just a funny-looking twig.

The reversal of this question, by the way, is one that asks: Is my impression of me different from the impression others have of me? Survival systems require that you not develop certain potentials to their fullest. In some cases, it also requires that self-awareness of potential be minimized or totally denied.

Others may see you as having special talents, intelligence, or physical abilities; but you will be unable to see these qualities in yourself.

An example of this is Diane from a previous chapter. When she was in college, neither her professors nor fellow students saw her as anything but bright and competent. Her sense of herself was quite the opposite, believing that she was not bright enough to pass the exams.

Point: The term "echo"—as used in this book—is a signal that someone is experiencing and repeating a pattern, as an adult, that was originally established in childhood. Jackie's "echoes" were used as specific examples to show how they worked and to emphasize their importance.

An "echo"—in its broadest sense—is what an individual can experience when a physical and/or psychological reaction to an event he or she had previously lived through is reignited by some action or emotion associated with the original experience. Think of the veteran who reacts to a loud bang after returning from a war experience—or an individual having experienced a major earthquake, reacting to the rumbling of an underground train. The difference between this general meaning of the word and its meaning in the context of a survival system is that an individual is not just reacting to the past, but unknowingly repeating a physical and psychological pattern established in childhood that was a response to the demands of another.

The dictionary defines an echo as a repetition of sound produced by the reflection of sound waves from a wall or other obstructing surface. Now, let's take Jackie's "echo" of assuming inappropriate responsibilities at work and put it into the above definition. A repetition of sound (Jackie's inappropriate responsibilities at work) produced (acted out) by the reflection of sound waves (by Jackie having had to assume inappropriate responsibilities as a child [because of]) from an obstructing surface (her mother's deafness). There was the "echo" of her not being able to say "no" at work because she had had no permission to say "no" to the needs of her mother and younger siblings. There was the echo of the myth of mother's hearing in the myth of brother's investments. There even was the echo of the silence of the adults in her childhood in the silence of her husband.

Thus the "echoes" of your past, reverberating in your present life, can act as major clues as to why you may have needed a survival system. Note that there are "echoes" in almost all of the case histories. Beth felt the echoes in the religious group she joined that had labeled her the spinster. Len felt the echo of his mother's intrusiveness in his wife's straightening out of his studio. Diane's echo of her cousins' teasing was the partner's putdowns. You will find other examples of echoes as you continue to read the rest of the histories.

Action: Pay attention to what doesn't feel right in your current life. It can be issues in your personal life, your business dealings, social interactions, or any activities with which you are involved. Look for consistent patterns such as: being ignored, being burdened, unfairly criticized, taken advantage of, called upon to rescue, expected to be perfect, expected to make everyone happy, expected to sacrifice for another, made to feel stupid, not respected, not trusted, being at the end of a yo-yo, and so on. Then analyze these patterns to see if they have any connection to how and what you were subjected to as a child. **If you catch an echo, follow it to its source.** Using Jackie as an example, her experience of being unfairly burdened and covering for others was a consistent pattern we first found in her work situation. Analyzing the pattern, she heard the echo in her playing the role of mother's ears, in order to maintain the myth of mother's hearing. Acknowledging that myth ultimately led to the discovery of the current myth surrounding her brother. And acknowledging the latest myth allowed her to free herself from the "seriousness" of her life.

Point: Understanding the pseudo-adult child. A friend of mine once casually made a remark that I never forgot. "I used to think," she said, "that I was so mature. Until I realized that I was only serious." Children who are given adult responsibilities prematurely often fall into this trap. They are usually in situations where the adults are unable and/or unwilling to appropriately handle responsibilities and require the child to become, what I call, a "pseudo-adult child." These are children who assume adult responsibilities but—still thinking in the concrete and egocentric ways of the child— get caught in distorted beliefs of what it means to assume adult responsibilities. Take the issue of time. For an adult, the designated time of a meeting has some flexibility given the vagaries of traffic, etc. The responsible adult would leave home early enough to arrive on time, but not be devastated if he/she were a few minutes late. The pseudo-adult child, thinking in absolutes, would feel a high degree of pressure to be at the meeting at the exact time, with no excuses for lateness accepted. For Jackie, the requirement to be her mother's ears demanded that she hear and report *every* word the clerk said, causing an extra dimension of the burden of mother's hearing loss. Labeling the behavior helped Jackie break the hold of needing to be so responsible.

The pseudo-adult child is often the designated "caretaker" of both the parent(s) and younger sibling(s). Most damaging is the need to be the "perfect" child, the child who never misbehaves, admits to having a problem, and never asks for help. These children grow up to be adults who associate being an adult with being serious and burdened and have internalized a belief that they have no permission to meet their own needs, only the needs of the other. Confusing play with immaturity, they internalized a belief that play was a negative activity, thus losing something valuable as adults. The capacity to play not only allows for relaxation and a reduction of stress, it fosters creativity and growth.

Action: Ask yourself if you assumed adult responsibilities too soon; felt that life was and is a burden; are caught in the trap of perfectionism; have unreasonable demands and expectations of yourself; and/or lack permission to play. If you answer yes, you may be caught in having needed to be a pseudo-adult child. It is time now to give yourself permission to become involved in activities that allow for greater flexibility and enjoyment. I will often suggest to patients who have been caught in systems that have restricted their play that they become involved in activities that they might like but never participated in. There are no age restrictions on such sports as baseball, tennis, swimming, and volleyball. I also encourage people to engage in activities such as dancing, fencing, acting, improvisational games, joining a chorus, learning a musical instrument, or any other experience that offers opportunities for much needed breaks from the responsibilities these people have assumed.

Point: A parent's need to maintain power over a child is a pervasive theme of survival systems. This stranglehold of power can serve a number of dysfunctional parental needs, including:

▸ needing to not let go of the child;

▸ needing to feel important;

▸ needing to be needed;

▸ needing to be the one and only authority;

▸ their own anxieties about their being abandoned;

▸ even needing to hold on to the fantasy that, if they continue to experience their children as young, so too are they.

As already mentioned, parents have their own reactions and adaptations to the traumas of their childhood.

Emily could only speculate as to why her father needed to keep her "a young, raw recruit, needing to follow orders." His own childhood environment had been difficult and his life in the military probably reinforced his controlling behavior. Her mother's pattern of interpreting and/or interceding with the father's actions reinforced the message that Emily was not capable of taking charge of her own life. Concurrent with that, and strongly reinforcing it, was the message that Emily must pay heed to what they said she should do, how she should feel, what she should think, and what she should want.

Action: Ask yourself if there is a discrepancy between what you have wanted to be or do and what others believe you should do. "Should" and "should not" are the key words. Emily's parents thought she *should not* become an artist—that she *should* seek security and *should* become a teacher. Her professor thought she *should* take German. Her husband thought she *should* be willing to sell the house. In Emily's world the "shoulds" carried the full power of authority. Non-compliance meant disapproval, arguments, even abandonment. Until her recognition of her survival system, Emily had gone along with all the "shoulds" in her life, the only exception being her response to the Vietnam War. Her parents' attacking reaction affirmed what she had always sensed would happen if she knew and expressed her own wants, thoughts, and opinions.

Unlike Emily, who went along with the orders, some children tend to react to a parent's need to control by developing a system that requires resistance to all forms of authority—a universal "No!" to what others believe they should do. This resistance extends, over time, to include the part of them that acts as their internal authority—the part that says, "you should" to many actions that would be beneficial. Have you said to yourself, "I really should exercise," and immediately respond negatively? How about asking yourself if you should give up smoking? Pay those bills? Do your income tax? You get the idea.

If you are in such a system, it is crucial that you learn to negotiate with yourself in order to minimize your automatic reaction to what you perceive as unwarranted authority.

Point: The actual environmental demand behind a "Snow White need" can be difficult to pin down. Emily's system serves as a good example of this. We had worked on the hypothesis that she needed to be unable to make a decision, which would lead to her not getting what she wanted. An unexpected revelation was the recognition that Emily's system was based on her *need not to **know** what she wanted, rather than on a need not to **decide** or a need to not **get** what she wanted.* Her need not to know what she wanted reinforced her parent's power, for the difference between her not being able to make a decision and her not knowing what she wanted created a greater adherence to her father's power. If Emily was caught only in indecision, her power to act would have been checkmated, but she would have retained some sense of her own power, albeit a limited one. In not knowing what she wanted, the power totally shifted to her parents who knew, without question, what she should want.

Action: Ask yourself if you would respond to a problem situation differently if you knew how you truly felt about how you wanted to deal with or solve the problem. In Emily's case, clearly knowing that she wanted to hold on to the house that she had always dreamed about, and that her husband wanted to sell, led to her taking a strong stand against the sale. This in turn led to her husband's refusal to compromise and the ultimate end of the marriage. The recognition of her feelings about the house was the beginning of her journey to break free from her hidden survival system.

Point: A need to not know is a familiar one in spy stories. The character slated to go into enemy territory is given only that information necessary for the success of the mission. Information not needed for the mission is not revealed to the character, for if she were to be caught, she could only reveal what she knew. Inherent in a survival system is a similar dynamic: the child who implicitly senses danger and adapts (Snow White needing to become ugly), needs not to consciously know the danger (stepmother's narcissism), for fear of the other's knowing (stepmother sensing that Snow White doesn't see her as the fairest of them all) and arousing a destructive reaction in the other (a murderous attack by the stepmother). Needing not to know thus sets up an additional protective barrier against a potential danger. Needing not to know is also a factor in not being blamed or not being held responsible.

Action: Don't get discouraged if you have difficulty in determining what your environmental demands and "Snow White needs" were. Survival systems, structured to be invisible and hidden, strongly resist attempts at being discovered—even under the scope of therapy. Remember, these systems represent implicit knowing and were established without the conscious awareness of the individual. To break the secret code of a system requires patience, tolerance, and respect for the survival needs of a child. In some cases it may require professional help.

Point: There can be other adaptations that a child uses to meet the parental need of maintaining power. Sam, now in his midthirties, serves as an example. He had been working for his father for a number of years, and it was understood that one day he would own the family business. His father, however, believed that Sam was not yet responsible enough to handle important tasks and would admonish Sam to "grow up and act like an adult." Sam, angry and resentful of his father's criticisms, reacted in many ways as an irresponsible and rebellious child, e.g., forgetting to deposit income receipts. His father's reaction would then focus on how Sam couldn't be trusted and given responsibilities. Sam, experiencing his father as once more treating him as a child, would respond accordingly. And so it went.

Sam began to ask: "Do I need, for some unknown reason, to be treated—*and behave*—as a child?" Slowly, he recognized that his father could not let go of the business and allow Sam to assume equal adult status. His father played out that need by continuing to treat Sam as a child, for as long as Sam was seen as irresponsible and untrustworthy, the father's ownership and authority could not be challenged. Sam unknowingly played an active part in the dynamic by continuing to act irresponsibly.

Action: Being able to be objective is a key attitude that can lead to insight and change. Without being critical or judgmental, ask yourself if you are unknowingly participating in an archaic pattern of adherence or resistance to inappropriate parental control. Your understanding of how the control is manifested and how you have continued to respond to it offers the solution to how you can change. In Sam's case, he learned to not react to his father's criticisms and paid close attention to following through on all of his duties and commitments. His father slowly relinquished more control; and Sam, recognizing his father's need, stayed the course until his father retired.

Point: The image of a mousetrap holding a ping-pong ball is a metaphor that dramatically captures the dynamic of negative interactions between two people. The image was first introduced in a film to explain the power of nuclear reaction. In the film, the setting is a room; all is quiet. Then a single ping-pong ball is tossed into the room—*the one and only action.*

After this action, what occurs is *all* reaction, with mousetraps springing their balls in response to being hit. In just a few seconds the room explodes in a snowstorm of bouncing ping-pong balls—

reaction> to greater reaction> to even greater reaction> to EXPLOSION!!!

The image of mousetraps holding ping-pong balls is useful and effective because it is an immediate and dramatic image of what's behind chronic negative interactions that continue to trap two people in gridlock and explosions. An individual can have an unresolved issue, a survival adaptation, or a childhood wound sitting inside his or her psyche, not unlike a mousetrap holding a ping-pong ball. When someone close to that individual has an internalized mousetrap/ping-pong ball as well, it takes only one action to set off an explosion. One person makes a comment that causes a reaction in the other. The other reacts and says something *as a result of that reaction*. The other reacts, or re-reacts, to that reaction, thus setting off a new round of reactions until, in a minute or two, there's an explosion.

As you saw in Emily's case, not being able to hold on to what she wanted because of her parents' dysfunctional needs was her issue and/or wound. Her husband had his own mousetrap and ping-pong ball setup that seemed to be related to his sense of his importance—or unimportance. Imagine this! Emily and John, each with her/his own internal mousetrap/ping-pong ball, are in a discussion. One of them—they take turns—throws just one ball. To spring Emily's ball, John simply needs not to meet Emily's needs or wants, or acknowledge her ideas. For John, Emily would simply need to make a comment making him feel unimportant. Remember, only one action is necessary.

Let's say Emily throws the first "ball." That causes John to react. Emily then reacts to John's reaction. And John reacts to Emily's last reaction. In a short time there is reaction upon reaction upon reaction, leading to an explosion.

Avoiding "nuclear reactions" requires several steps:

- each party needs to begin to recognize what the hidden issue of his/her childhood is (the ping-pong ball the mousetraps might be holding);

- each party needs to become sensitive to the mousetraps/ping-pong balls of the other and how each individual sets off the reaction of the other;

- the parties must establish agreed signals—using verbal and nonverbal signs and gestures—to signal that the mousetraps are about be set off or, having been set off, are heading for an explosion;

- move to a "time-out" to let both parties separate and cool down.

It is important to understand that these "mousetraps" of childhood are often well hidden and do not give up their power easily. But gaining control over your automatic reactions offers the very special gift of healthy relationships free of destructive explosions.

Action: Recognizing the wounds of your childhood is one of the more difficult challenges in the process of breaking free from the past. It means acknowledging that, as a child, you lost all or part of your childhood. That loss is painful—a deep wound, deeply buried. And like all wounds, it continues to fester until it is exposed and allowed to heal. Cluing in to what painful experiences may be inside the "ball" your inner "mouse-trap" is holding is the first step. As we saw in the previous case of Diane and her effective use of her anxiety reactions, the recognition and use of a negative reaction can lead to positive results. Pay attention to what seems to be overreactions or chronic mini-explosions between you and your partner. Take the time to spot the consistent issues leading to the reaction and then "follow" the reaction to its source.

CHAPTER SIXTEEN

A Poorness-of-Fit

Peter was a unique combination of contrasts. He had an air of sophistication, yet seemed rather unworldly. He had a potential for good looks, yet his skin tone was pale and pasty. His tall, thin, flexible body could be that of a dancer, yet he moved in a stiff, awkward manner. He was clearly intelligent and articulate, yet had a stilted, dull speaking style. He seemed to have a high level of energy, yet there was something flat about him.

The Need to Not Feel: Peter

Peter seemed to have it all. A compatible twenty-four-year marriage. Two healthy, almost-grown children. A flourishing business based on one of his inventions. A beautiful home. An income that allowed him to buy "toys" like the classic cars he enjoyed owning. Even the prestige of an unused PhD in physics.

There was, however, one crucial element missing—his capacity to feel. As he explained in his first session, he believed he had everything but a true sense of himself and a real connection to his feelings.

174

"My father died," he said, "and I felt nothing. My older brother died and I felt nothing. I almost died a few months ago of the same disease that killed my brother. Sure I was afraid, but other than fear, I felt nothing. That's when I decided to get some help." He was silent. "My brush with death made me realize how much of life I was missing."

I had little doubt that he was caught in a survival system. But I could not guess how powerful a system it was and how difficult it would be for him to break free.

As Peter shared his history, I became aware that he not only lacked a sense of connection to himself, but also suffered a profound disconnection from others. The only exception to his alienation seemed to be his immediate family, consisting of his wife and two children. It was as if, for him, the four of them existed on a remote island. The family members themselves didn't appear to share this isolation, wife and children all leading active social lives.

Peter moved in a social world but seemed untouched by it. Or perhaps, he would not allow it to touch him. The second possibility appeared more accurate, and I noticed that his stiff and unyielding posture created an immediate sense of distance between us and he would bend his body away from me whenever he had to pass by to enter the room.

Peter had not lived the typical life of an American child. He, his mother, older brother, and younger sister had followed the father, a geologist working for a large oil company, to various global assignments, living in South America, Canada, Germany, India, and Australia. Between assignments, the family would live in the United States for a few months to several years at a time.

This nomadic existence partially explained his sense of not belonging. His kindergarten year was spent in Germany, where he attended a school for the children of British soldiers. During the family's four-year stay in India, he had socialized primarily with children of British colonials. And while living in Australia, the family had been stationed in a remote area where simply being an American made him different. By his early teens, he was a sophisticated world traveler who did not fit into the provincial world of a small-town American high school. But it was clear from his recollections of those years that he had enjoyed much of his life in these different countries. No, I thought, his sense of being an outsider didn't originate in the family's travels.

Family photographs are useful in revealing hidden dynamics among family members, and I had asked Peter to bring in whatever he had. We found our first clue in a black and white photograph of Peter, his father, mother, brother, and sister. His father and mother are standing behind his brother and sister, all four of them looking to the right. Peter, standing a foot-and-half away from the others, is looking in the opposite direction.

Peter was both surprised and not surprised by the photograph. He was surprised to see, in black and white, what he had known—but had not felt—growing up. Not surprised, because the photo concretized his sense of apartness and alienation from his family. What was striking for me was to see the split between what he *knew* and what he *felt*. He accepted proof of his alienation from the family as just another "thing" to know. The absence of feelings minimized its importance.

In Peter's case, the consequence of not feeling a part of his family was particularly significant. The family's travels had interfered with his being able to establish a bond with any group, particularly a peer group. And not being a part of the only group that was consistent left him with a chronic sense of being an outsider. It was not until he entered college in northern California that he began to experience a sense of belonging.

To my questions of why he might have needed to separate himself from his family, Peter would respond with a simple, "I don't know. I never thought about it before." Until he started therapy, it had never occurred to him to think about the world of his childhood. Because no feelings were attached to his memories, he categorized them as unimportant or meaningless.

And so we began to "think" about his history.

Peter's mother came from a small college town in Ohio, one of three children of two college professors. She had met Peter's father in New York City where she had hoped to begin an acting career. Her career had never materialized, and she had devoted her time and energy to her husband and children.

Peter's father was the only son of an Orthodox Jewish family. Marrying outside his religion guaranteed a lifelong estrangement from his family. To me it raised the question of whether his father had needed to rebel against his family; and, if so, was that a connection to Peter's also needing to be an outsider?

I asked Peter if his father ever talked about his being Jewish and if anyone outside of the immediate family was aware of it. His answer to both questions was "No."

"Do you think it might have been an issue for your father?" I asked. "Particularly since he was working in an industry and in locales that, at that time, were probably anti-Semitic."

"I never thought about that," Peter replied, "and I doubt that even if I had, I would have questioned my father."

"Why not?" I asked.

"It was not a subject we discussed," he answered.

We speculated about how Peter's father might have felt about his situation and whether his being Jewish had made any difference in his professional life or personal life. Our speculations went nowhere.

Peter did report that both parents were heavily invested in his older brother's academic achievements. "That actually was an advantage for me," Peter said. "It took the pressure off me, particularly since my grades weren't great."

At this point we had sketched a fairly accurate but superficial picture of the family members, including his younger sister. What continued to elude us were the forces that had caused Peter to need to develop his survival system.

One day Peter, who was usually focused about whatever we were discussing, seemed preoccupied and a bit edgy.

I asked him if anything was wrong.

"No," he answered. "It's just that my weekly phone conversations with my mother occasionally get to me."

I asked him what she said that bothered him.

"It's what she doesn't say that bothers me," he answered. "She's so blank, so disinterested and uninvolved. She sits in that dark apartment, goes nowhere, sees no one, and watches television all day. I know she loves her grandchildren, but she never asks about them. And even when I tell her about some special thing they've done, she doesn't get excited or even seem particularly interested."

I asked him how old his mother was.

"She's in her seventies," he replied.

"She sounds like she might be suffering from depression," I suggested. "After all, she's lost her husband and a son."

"No," Peter answered emphatically. "She's *always* been like that—way before my brother and father died."

And Peter began to describe an individual who fit the diagnostic profile of chronic clinical depression. She had been unhappy, unenthusiastic, and uninterested in anything but the school grades of her older son. According to Peter, she was remote, lacked energy, and spent hours reading.

There was no sense in asking Peter how he had "felt" about his mother's depression since he lived in his head. But I could see by his reaction to those phone calls that this was fertile territory to explore.

Again, we found a clue in a photograph. In this one, Peter is about six or seven years old, all skinny arms and legs, with a great big grin on his face. There is an energy and exuberance that jumps out of the photograph. I commented on that exuberance.

"My mother told me," he said, looking at the picture, "that I was always wandering off. I vaguely remember wandering off in an airport once when I was about four or five. That must have given her quite a jolt."

As I looked at that picture, I'm not sure for whom I felt more sympathy, Peter or his mother. He must have been a pistol, I thought: a skinny, high-energy boy, brimming with curiosity, lacking fear, and ready to take on any challenge. What an incredible lack of "fit" between them. One could imagine the hidden vibrations between the boy in the picture and his depressed, lethargic mother.

We spent a number of sessions exploring how the "poorness-of-fit" might have affected him. It was clear that his brother, who was a quiet, compliant, and studious child, would have been more compatible with their mother's limitations. The much younger sister was treated as the "baby" of the family. Our exploration of the effects of the poor mother/son fit soon uncovered a key word, inappropriate. Not understanding the innate temperament of this child, his mother had responded to his behaviors and actions as being inappropriate. It was inappropriate to wander off, to run when one could walk, to not study one's lessons, to be tardy, to ask too many questions, to have too much exuberance, and so on. The powerful message Peter internalized was that he could not trust himself to know what was acceptable behavior and what actions would be criticized and ridiculed. The poor fit between his nature and the style of the British school he had attended while in India reinforced his sense of his unacceptability and inappropriateness.

How then was he able to successfully establish a marriage in spite of his survival system? Peter had enrolled in a college that was known for its academic excellence. A special benefit, he discovered, was the freedom and energy of the student body. At last he had found a right "fit" and, for the first time in his life, he was compatible with his environment. The woman he married was a part of that world. His system was reactivated when he left that environment, but the freedom he felt with her remained.

His new insights were helping him to feel a little more comfortable in the world of people, but Peter was still living in his head, still far from experiencing his feelings, and still holding his body as if he were on military parade. Maybe he could get at his system by working on easing his physical stiffness.

We started to discuss what steps he could take for that purpose, including an exercise program.

"I already work with a trainer," he replied, "and I've been doing yoga for over a year."

Both activities, it seemed to me, required little direct and active interaction with another person. And neither offered an opportunity to express physical spontaneity. "How about trying some dance lessons?" I suggested.

At first Peter was reluctant but decided to take a risk by signing up for tango lessons. His teacher's comments about his stiffness and reluctance to take the initiative with his partner reinforced much of what we had talked about in our sessions. To Peter's credit, he stayed with the lessons.

Shortly after the tango lessons began, we discovered one of the ways Peter maintained his defense against feelings. The clue was a momentary change in his stilted, precise, and unemotional style of speaking. It was a style that could be defensive but also one that was a result of his training as a scientist.

We had been working together for over a year, and I began to wonder if we had gone as far as we could. I believe he picked up on my unspoken resignation, for he unexpectedly cried out one day:

"Don't give up on me. Please, *don't give up*." His plea touched me deeply. and I assured him that I would not give up.

I was struck by the contrast between how he had spoken those words and how he usually communicated. Those words held feelings, passion, and spontaneity. They were impulsive, unguarded, and very real. His usual controlled, unemotional style was the exact opposite. Is he somehow programming himself? Does his speech sound so guarded because of a gap between his thoughts and how and what he says? Do his thoughts and feelings go through some kind of an internal monitoring device that acts like a censoring machine? To all those questions, the answer was "Yes."

We had uncovered a key element in the protective wall he had built around himself as a child. "You mean," Peter said, "I have found a clue to the structure of my tank. That tank you talk about that children build when they are in a war zone."

"Yes," I answered. "But remember, the child doesn't build an escape hatch that allows him to move freely in a world of peace."

I told Peter that I was impressed with his tank's ability to protect him. But *what* was he protecting and *from whom*? The dynamic between Peter and his mother did not seem negative enough to have warranted such a powerful protective system. We took another look at his father.

He once had described an early memory of his father nagging him to eat the food on his plate. We started there. "Nagging" became "insisting," which became "demanding," which became "shouting," which became a memory of five-year old Peter sitting for hours at the table, a plate of uneaten food in front of him.

"That wasn't about food," I said. "That was about control."

"I really didn't like my father very much," Peter said. "He always seemed to be yelling at me. I guess there was as bad a fit between my father and myself as there had been between me and my mother." And he was right. His father had been angry and insensitive, spewing a steady stream of demeaning criticism at his younger son.

"I think my father took pleasure in humiliating me," Peter said.

I asked him what he remembered.

"When I was in college," he answered, "I was getting A's in all my subjects except French. Somehow, languages were difficult for me. My father would ignore my good grades and find ways of broadcasting my one academic failing."

"Yes," I said, "but what about the earlier times? When you were a child. How would he humiliate you then?" There was a long pause.

"I can't seem to remember," Peter answered.

"Or perhaps it's too painful to remember," I replied.

We speculated that possibly his father believed that Peter's energy and fearlessness needed to be curbed in order for him to survive a world that the father saw as dangerous. Or maybe Peter, who looked very much like his father, was the target of the older man's internalized self-hate. Or perhaps he was just an authoritarian and angry individual. In any case, we now knew against whom the tank was built.

But *what* was it that Peter needed to protect? It clearly was something intrinsic and core to his existence, yet something well hidden. He kept his distance from his mother in order not to get caught in her chronic depression. And he had to protect himself from his father's domination. But why did he need not to feel? We both knew that an important piece of the puzzle was still missing, that his reflection still wasn't clear.

And then Peter's fourteen-year-old dog died.

Responding to the work we had been doing, the hatch on his "tank" opened, at least for a while, and his feelings of sadness and loss came pouring out. What also came out of hiding was his true, emotional nature. Insignificant clues came together to form a picture of a man innately responsive, highly sensitive, and keenly empathetic. Someone who, as a child, had become a vegetarian because "people shouldn't kill living things." No wonder he had been able to sense my doubts about being able to help him.

It was clear that the interaction between a boy with such heightened sensitivity and his parents, who were struggling with their own demons, would have inspired an unusually powerful need for a survival system.

"It must have been terribly difficult for you," I said. "No wonder you shut off your feelings and so many of your memories. Your survival system was protecting your essence, your soul."

Peter nodded his head but said nothing. I think he was close to tears but was not yet ready to completely let his guard down in front of me.

The hatch on his tank closed down after a few days. But we now knew what his system had been protecting and against whom. If he had not "ducked," his sensitive core would have been destroyed by his father's attacks. And his empathetic nature would have been overwhelmed by his mother's unhappiness.

Our next challenge was how to more effectively dismantle a system as creatively designed and long-lasting as his. To Peter's question of how to achieve this, I could only answer, "Slowly and with difficulty." I cautioned Peter not to underestimate the power of a well-constructed survival system. A "tank" like his would have to be dismantled with kindness, gentleness—and a great deal of creativity.

Peter's choice of learning the tango was a creative beginning to the dismantling of his system. Dancing offered him a safe arena to begin to free his body from its stiffness and to feel more comfortable in expressing his energy and exuberance. Each lesson in which he experienced himself differently was slowly silencing the power of the voices that had criticized what they had seen as his inappropriate behavior.

Peter mentioned recently that he and his wife were planning a trip to Argentina to take tango lessons with a special teacher.

There is more of Peter showing every day.

CHAPTER SEVENTEEN

The Interaction

The Interaction, as the third element of a survival system, relates to the congruence or lack of it, between the child's personality and the environment in which the child lives. A good fit between these two variables is a key factor in an individual reaching his or her potential. A poor fit can play a crucial role in the child's need for a survival adaptation.

Interaction has two meanings, one that relates to the development of individuality and one that relates to the interplay between an individual and his or her environment. For many years, the concept of "individuality" was wrapped in a "nature versus nurture" dynamic, with the individual caught between these two conflicting influences. The present understanding of individuality is of the continual reciprocal action between the uniqueness of an individual and his or her early childhood environment. Think of it as a kind of weaving between the biology of the individual and his or her very early experiences, resulting in a "cloth of individuality; thus individuality reflects the dynamic interplay of some characteristics of that individual and some variables of that early environment.

The interaction, as the third element of a survival system however, has a more specific meaning and can itself be the source of an adaptive need. The congruence—or lack of it—between the child's personality and the personality and parenting practices of the parents can play a crucial role in the child's need for survival adaptation. As we have seen in the last section, some environments can be so distorting that most children, regardless of their personality, will react either directly or with an adaptive system. But in some cases, the damaging effect is in the quality and nature of the interaction and not inherent in the environment itself.

Research began to focus on the temperament of infants and young children more than forty-five years ago, with the work of Alexander Thomas and Stella Chess. Their focus was twofold: to explore a possible connection between early temperament and the development of psychopathology; and to offer what information they could to pediatricians and parents. The results of their research formed the basis for much of current parenting literature, including the phrase "goodness-of-fit" to describe the child/parent interaction. What they observed is that the congruence between the child's temperament and the parents' attitudes and practices can determine future psychological growth. According to their findings, if there is a goodness-of-fit, the child's development will be enhanced and lead to what Thomas and Chess call a healthy personality structure. On the other hand, should there be a poorness-of-fit, the researchers believed that the basis would be set for unhealthy personality structures or pathological symptoms.

According to the requirements of the survival system approach, if there is a goodness-of-fit there will not be a need for a survival system. When, however, there is a negative discrepancy between the individuality of the child and the child's environment, the poorness-of-fit can result in a survival system. This system can easily be misinterpreted as an unhealthy personality or pathological development.

The shift from pathology to adaptation is a key component of the survival system approach and one of the reasons it can be so effective in facilitating change. As long as certain behaviors and beliefs are seen as "pathological" and not as having been appropriately adaptive to a childhood environment, an accurate understanding of the problem is not possible. And without such an understanding, change is limited.

The interaction factor also explains why two or more children raised in the same family and influenced by the same environment can have very different behaviors, beliefs, and degrees of functioning.

Some conflicts of personality and parenting styles between parent and child are particularly damaging and consequently more conducive to a child's needing a survival system. These include:

- risk-taking child with a fearful parent—possible survival system:

  a need to deny any and all danger;

- high-energy child with a depressed parent—possible survival system:

  a need to be constrained;

- anxious child with an angry parent—possible survival system:

  a need to be perfect;

- stubborn child with a controlling parent—possible survival system:

  a need to say "no" to any and all "shoulds";

- timid child with an aggressive parent—possible survival system:

  a need to be invisible;

- low-persistence child with an ambitious parent— possible survival system:

  a need to fail;

- shy child with a highly sociable parent—possible survival system:

  a need to hide.

The message parents can send when there is a poorness-of-fit is that something is "wrong" with the child, rather than there is something "wrong" with the congruence between them. Once set, the initial poorness-of-fit experience is often perpetuated in school experiences, social groups, and professional choices.

The nature of the fit between individuals and their environment is not limited to parent/child interactions. There can also be a goodness- versus poorness-of-fit between an individual and the practices and beliefs of his or her family's culture or group. This is particularly powerful when the family continues to identify with its primary group while the child reaches out, through school and other activities, to establish a connection to the values, language, and practices of a more mainstream culture. The congruence then between the child, now increasingly integrated into a new culture, and the static nature of the family's group becomes increasingly strained.

CHAPTER EIGHTEEN

Fixing the Fit

POINTS TO MAKE
ACTIONS TO TAKE

Point: The poorer the fit, the greater is the need for a stronger, more protective survival system. Peter had one of the strongest, most resistant systems I have encountered because there were three separate forces driving Peter's need for a survival system: his own sensitive and empathetic nature, his mother's long-standing depression, and his father's controlling and negative behaviors. It is questionable whether Peter would have developed and maintained as powerful an adaptive system had any one of these three been missing. A less sensitive and empathetic child would be less likely to have been so strongly affected by either the mother or the father. Conversely, Peter, remaining the same sensitive person, would not have needed to live so completely in his head had he been dealing with only one difficult parent.

Action: Explore the goodness-of-fit versus the poorness-of-fit between you and your world. Maintaining as much objectivity as you can, evaluate your personality and emotional nature and do the same for your parents. Ask yourself if there seems to be a conflict between your basic temperament and personality and that of your parents in your current interactions with them. Since personality and emotional nature tend to remain stable over time, who you are and who your parents are now should act as a guide to the nature of the fit when you were a child.

Point: Photographs can be valuable clues to the past. Peter's need for a survival system was captured in the two photographs he brought in. The first, showing him standing apart from his family, was symbolic of his alienation from them. The second, and more important one, was where his energy and exuberance as a child bursts through to the viewer, revealing the "true" Peter. Unfortunately, his parents experienced this Peter as being the "inappropriate" child rather than their having limited parenting skills.

An associate of mine was once asked to evaluate a young boy who was showing signs of withdrawal and depression. The results of an extensive evaluation confirmed that the boy had a very negative sense of himself and a good deal of internal confusion. No obvious reason for his emotional state could be found—until his mother brought in the family album. In all of the family pictures, the central figure that the camera focused on was not the child but the family dog—a big, furry sheepdog that had been the parents' special "baby" since they had first met. The boy was confused and sad because he experienced the dog as a favored older "sibling."

Action: Photographs of an individual as a young child often capture the fundamental essence of that person before environmental demands have taken their toll. Remember Jackie, who needed to be the "ears" of her mother? She found a photograph of herself at age six taken before all of her younger siblings were born, before she began carrying the full weight of her responsibilities. The camera had caught her dancing on the lawn, her arms outstretched and her feet off the ground.

It was a picture of joy and freedom.

Find a photo of yourself as a child that reflects your true inner self. Enlarge it, frame it, and place it within easy view. View this picture as representing your potential, your inherent aliveness, your hidden self.

Look through your family albums and notice the way people relate to each other: do they touch, not touch, touch inappropriately, look in the same direction, stand apart, include or exclude certain members.

Point: The metaphor of "a tank in a war zone" can be useful, especially for men, when pursuing the how and why of a survival system. Imagine what it would feel like to be a child in a war zone. In order to survive you would have to avoid getting hit by bullets, bombs, or other kinds of weaponry. What, you would ask yourself, is the greatest protection against this happening? A tank, you would answer, having seen war movies—a tank so thick and solid that nothing could penetrate its protective walls. But when you left the war zone (childhood), you would be stuck in that tank. Remember, we don't build our tanks with escape hatches.

Or perhaps, because of your gentle and sensitive nature, instead of a tank in response to a war zone, you would disappear into the walls and become invisible. After all, if you can't see me, you can't shoot me. You then spend years as an adult, hoping to be noticed but remaining someone whom nobody seems to remember.

Action: Since every tank is custom-made, building an escape hatch requires some creative insights and innovative actions. Comments by friends as to how they experience you can be a useful beginning. In Peter's case, my comments about how he moved in a stiff and stilted way offered a clue to his being trapped in a "tank." His willingness to take tango lessons and risk changing how he existed within his body was the beginning of his finding his escape hatch. Other characteristics associated with living in a tank can include, among others: an aura of being untouchable; inflexibility in both body and verbal language; a strong tendency to "run over" ideas and people; and disparaging remarks acting as a "first strike."

For those caught in being invisible, a clue is the consistency of being overlooked, not remembered and inadvertently not invited, or any experience of not being recognized. Behaviors that result in your avoiding being the appropriate object of attention or focus are worth analyzing for their adaptive meaning.

Point: Dismantling an adaptive system requires more than uncovering, understanding, and just talking about the original need for it. Survival systems are protective and as such may have stifled some aspect of your personality or required your limiting some part of your emotional, social, or intellectual growth. For example, Peter's body stiffness was the result of his need to keep tight control over all of his actions. The fear of being inappropriate resulted in his minimizing and stifling his natural exuberance. Taking dance lessons offered him an opportunity to be in an environment that encouraged freedom of movement.

Action: Ask yourself if your system has prevented you from reaching your potential by consistently stifling or negating physical, social, or intellectual opportunities. An example would be the woman who became the silent child. Her ability and confidence to speak in class was severely curtailed because of her childhood need not to reveal family secrets. Her recognition that she was not sure how to pronounce words and that she lacked confidence in being able to articulate her ideas allowed her to take action in rectifying this liability. This included taking speech classes, including one focusing on public speaking.

Your challenge is to figure out what you lack and what activities or experiences would fill that gap. Be aware that you may have some built-in resistance for these activities, since these new experiences would be challenging the old system.

Point: When a poorness-of-fit between parent and child is particularly strong, the creation of a protective survival system can ensure the child's inner core remaining intact. Reacting directly to the negative vibrations of a poor fit often leads to more serious consequences. As an example of this, let me introduce Fred.

Fred's father remembered his own college football triumphs with great pride and looked forward to having a strong, fearless son who would "follow in his father's football footsteps." Fred, however, took after his mother's side of the family. Physically he was thin, emotionally he was sensitive, and his natural talent was in music, not sports. Fred felt the "vibrations" of his father's disappointment in him and internalized them as his father's anger at the defectiveness of his son. Thinking as a child, Fred didn't say, "My father lives in his past glories." He believed, "My father is disappointed in me because I'm such a failure and wimp."

Had Fred, as a child, developed a survival system, he might have done what Peter did—cut himself off from his feelings. In his case, however, Fred reacted directly to his father's vibrations and escaped from his feelings of self-hate by turning to drugs. He got hooked on heroin and still struggles with that addiction.

Action: No action is necessary—just an appreciation of your system and how it might have kept you safe.

PART THREE

Breaking Free from a Survival System

CHAPTER NINETEEN

The Life You Save May Be Your Own

NINE STEPS TO THE LIGHT SIDE OF THE MOON

The time has come for you to complete your journey to the light side of the moon. Try now to more fully answer the crucial question:

Do I need, for some unknown reason, to

_____?

In so doing, you will have an invaluable tool in your understanding of why you have been unable to reach your potential. All of the people you've met in this book were asked or asked themselves that question—over and over again. And as you work through breaking free, you will need to ask yourself that same question—over and over again.

This chapter focuses on the nine steps you can take to help free yourself from a hidden survival system. It asks you a series of questions, the answers to which can act as a guide

197

in first uncovering the adaptive behaviors and beliefs of your childhood and, secondly, in redirecting your efforts to change. Steps One and Two are questions that focus on whether you are, indeed, caught in a survival system based on how you feel about your present life and how the environment of childhood can lead to a need for adaptive survival. Steps Three, Four, Five, and Six are devoted to the three basic elements of a survival system as they specifically relate to you and how you can avoid misconceptions about them. Step Seven relates to the power of the system to resist any change, and Steps Eight and Nine offer a review of the techniques and suggestions to counteract that power.

Step 1. A Look at Your Present Life

Let's start with questions relating to how you feel about the quality of your life. Ask yourself:

> *Is there a discrepancy between what I*
> *want and what I am able to get?*

> *Is there a discrepancy between who I*
> *think I am and who I want to be?*

> *Do I feel that I'm living only half a life?*

> *Do I long to be free of some unknown burden I carry?*

> *Do I continue to behave in ways that defeat my goals?*

An affirmative answer to one or more of these questions points to a pattern of behavior and a belief system that may be acting as a barrier to your achieving your potential and marks the possible presence of a survival system. Many of the patients I have worked with over the years, and all of those mentioned in the previous chapters, had said, "yes," to all or some of these questions.

Before you assume that you are caught in an archaic adaptation, here are some general questions:

Will an unhappy childhood necessarily lead
to my having to cope with either the effects of
a trauma or a hidden survival system?

The answer is no, although it is difficult to escape a difficult childhood without some negative repercussions. How you are affected by the experiences of your childhood depends on a number of variables, such as: your temperament, personality, and emotional nature; your birth order; the specifics of what made your environment difficult; the interaction between your uniqueness and the world around you; and the counteracting effects of positive forces you might have experienced, including supportive relatives, friends, teachers, and other significant influences.

Is there a difference between behaviors and/
or emotional states that are the result of directly
experiencing a difficult/dangerous childhood
environment (taking a hit) and behaviors that acted
as protection against that environment (ducking)?

The behavior may or may not be the same. Certain states of being, such as confusion, indecision, and anxiety, lend themselves to being either a reactive or an adaptive response. What is key to being able to answer this question is uncovering the true reality of your childhood. If your negative state of being is the result of taking a hit, it is most likely that you will have clear memories of any traumas. There is also a good chance that you will get encouragement in your struggle to recover. If, however, your state of being is an adaptation against something or someone in your childhood environment, then your attempts to change are often stalled or defeated and your awareness of the potential traumas remains hidden. The repetitive, irrational, and seemingly illogical patterns of survival system beliefs and behaviors all share a common trait: their intractability is related to the hidden survival value they once served, even as they appear to keep us from getting what we say we want. But recognizing the adaptive nature of the behavior offers hope of change.

Are there clear signs or signals that point to
the existence of a hidden survival system?

There are no clear and specific signs that point to a survival system. One of the primary demands of a system is that it remain hidden and unrecognized. If, however, your answer to how you feel about your present life includes such words as stuck, frustrated, blocked, stymied, stopped, limited—and variations thereof—you may indeed be caught in a survival system.

A possible sign that a system exists is when the word *discrepancy* becomes a major theme. Notice that the first two questions in "Step 1. A Look at Your Present Life" is about discrepancies. Is there a discrepancy between what I want and what I am able to get? Is there a discrepancy between who I think I am and who I want to be? One can frame that question using other examples, such as: Is there a discrepancy between how others see me versus how I see myself; between my being articulate in some situations and struggling to speak in other situations; between how effective I am when doing for others versus doing for myself; between what I give and what I get in return? The presence of one or more discrepancies should be noted and explored for its meaning in the context of a survival system.

Step 2. A Look at the Danger

Let's first look at danger as it relates to survival. Ask yourself:

*Am I clear about the principles and theory of
Darwinian survival as it relates to me?*

Survival means remaining alive. The snowshoe hare that doesn't turn white in winter will not survive. Turning white is not under the conscious control of the animal but rather, according to Darwin's theory, due to the evolutionary laws of nature that deal with species' survival. The basic concept of this book proposes that the principles of Darwinian theory, as they relate to the human species, be expanded in two important ways. Just as a species will adapt to its physical environment in order to survive, so, accordingly, will human beings, with their higher consciousness, adapt to a psychological environment. And what is true for the human species is true, as well, for an individual human being.

Do I understand the power of attachment?

Attachment refers to the relationship that forms between infants/young children and their parents or parent substitutes. It is the bond that, at the most basic evolutionary level, allows the child to survive by seeking proximity to those who offer safety and comfort. It is the bond that allows the child to survive, physically and psychologically, for no young child can exist in isolation and without adult involvement. Imagine how it would feel if you were an astronaut walking on the moon and the "mother ship" headed back to Earth without you. That's the power of attachment. Because survival systems are developed in childhood, it is essential that you answer most of the questions that follow from a child's point of view. Begin by asking:

Do I understand how children think, feel,
and experience their world?

As discussed in Chapter Two, a factor in children believing that they need a survival system is how they interpret the behaviors of the adults in their world. Remember, a child's thinking is tied to an appropriate level of intellectual development, and young children think concretely. They do not understand the subtleties of language and assume a literal meaning of words.

Children believe that their parents are all-knowing and all-powerful. Since parents know everything, including their child's feelings and wants, a child may assume that his or her parents' lack of responsiveness is not because they don't know, but because they don't care. This trust in the perfection of parents reinforces children's belief that if anything is wrong, it must be with them and not the parents.

Children are egocentric, which translates into, "It's all about me!" This belief is not about vanity or self-aggrandizement but about how they believe, think, and question how they exist in their worlds. Their egocentricity leads them to believe that they are the center of their worlds and, as such, have imaginary powers to affect those worlds.

Review Chapter Three on how children understand their world to better understand how you, as a child, might have experienced your world.

Do I understand the concept of the "good-enough
mother" and "whose needs got met"?

Winnicott used the phrase "good-enough mother" to mean that the mother establishes an environment in which her infant can thrive by providing satisfaction *in response to the infant's signals*. If the mother has not been "good-enough" and substitutes her own gesture, the infant's sense of self is distorted. Substituting her own gesture would include such responses as being too busy to respond in a reasonable time, not understanding the infant's signal, and anticipating and meeting a perceived need of the infant *before* the infant can signal. This last one is what I call the "good mother."

The survival system approach expands the question— "Whose need got met?" well beyond the mother/infant dynamic. It asks the question in the context of a child's development through the critical years between early childhood and adolescence. It includes the influence of not only mothers who impose their needs on a child but fathers, siblings, other family members, and the entire range of influences upon a child.

> *Do you find it difficult, demoralizing, or*
> *strangely unnerving to be alone?*

The writings of Winnicott also offer a possible answer to this question.

In an insightful article entitled "The Capacity to Be Alone" he captured an essential quality of the parenting process. This capacity, according to the author, results from appropriate and supportive parenting and is an important indicator of a child's inner security. According to Winnicott, the ability to be comfortably alone is closely related to emotional maturity. The child develops the capacity to be alone when the child is allowed to be alone in the *presence* of a supportive parent.

For example, a child in a new situation is becoming involved in an unfamiliar activity; suddenly realizes he is separate from his parent; immediately looks around with a look of panic; sees the parent who acknowledges him with a supporting smile—but does not engage him—and the child goes back to playing and discovering new experiences. Had the parent not been there, the child would have immediately stopped his own activities and looked for the missing parent. Had the parent misinterpreted the child's look and actively engaged the child directly, the child's capacity to be alone would have been compromised. The parent who encourages the child to stay with his own explorations in separate space offers that child a wonderful gift of inner security.

As most of the case histories in this book have shown, a survival system is in response to the demands of another. In trying to understand the origin of your system, the first question you are encouraged to ask is: Do you, for some unknown reason, need to _____? The answer to whose needs got met offers possibilities for discovering the "unknown reason." Asking about needs getting met also raises the important questions of how, when, or even if your needs were met as a child.

The next question encourages you to ask about the possible negative consequences that would have occurred had you not developed your system. One way of teasing out the answer is to ask:

> *If I had a magic wand and could make my*
> *wants a reality, what would change? And would*
> *there be any danger if the magic worked?*

As we have seen, a survival system is in response to the needs and demands of someone or something else, with your needs and wants being secondary. Your asking about the possibility of having your wants met can point to who or what might have been, or still is, the "other." Using a magic wand offers a safe journey through what had been dangerous territory.

Imagine that the genie comes out of the bottle and grants your wish of making your "wants" a reality. Would there be any danger or serious consequences if that wish were to be fulfilled—assuming that you are still a child? In Beth's case, getting her wish to be free to live her own life caused a permanent break in her relationship with her father. As an adult, Beth could handle her father's rage; as a child she would have been devastated.

Keep in mind that survival systems represent what you, as a child, believed you needed to do in order to survive. Sometimes your belief was rooted in reality; sometimes it was due to a distortion of reality. In any case, the "environmental demand" was real to you, and the enduring power of a survival system rests in its internalized survival value. If a behavior, belief, or attitude has been internalized as necessary for your survival, then change will feel like a threat to your life.

Step 3. A Look at You

Since survival systems are the result of the interaction between one's uniqueness and one's childhood environment, there can be innumerable subtle differences in the resulting "custom-made" system. In answering the following questions, keep in mind your inherent personality and emotional nature and how they may have played a part in your having developed a survival system.

These are questions that ask you to look at yourself in a new and different way.

When I look in a mirror, is the reflection of my
physical image positive or negative?

Survival systems do not foster the development of positive self-esteem. If you are caught in one, there is a good possibility that you will find fault with your face and body image. The challenge is to tease out what lies behind that negative reflection. You could be looking at yourself through the distorted vision of others and their requirement that you not realize your physical potential. Snow White would be an example of this.

You could be seeing yourself through your own biases based on a false premise. Mark's belief of being *too much* is an example of this. Or you could be seeing yourself negatively in comparison to the prevailing "look" of your family or your culture—as did blond, green-eyed Sally. Look to see if you are revealing your hidden survival system as it is expressed in your physical appearance and carriage/the way you carry yourself.

Now explore your impression of "who" really lives in that reflection by asking:

How would I describe my personality
and emotional nature?

Various dimensions of personality and emotional tendencies, along with their expression in behaviors and moods, were discussed. These include the higher-order dimensions of positive emotionality, negative emotionality, constraint, activity level, and agreeableness/openness to experience. Take the time to review them and consider how they might have played a part in your responding to the demands of your environment. Remember, individuals who need to develop a survival system will respond to their environment in keeping with their characteristic personality and emotional style.

Is my impression of "me" different from
the impression others have of me?

Maintaining a survival system requires that you keep intact the distortions and discrepancies associated with it. In this question the distortion relates to self-awareness. Others may see you as having special talents, intelligence, or physical abilities; but you will be unable to see or experience these qualities in yourself. Diane's experience in college is an example of this. Her professors and other students saw her as very bright even as she continued to believe that she would fail. Take seriously the comments you get from friends and associates that seem to contradict the way you feel about yourself.

*Do I feel that there is a different
"me" waiting to be free?*

The "me" of a survival system can be quite different than the "me" of my potential. The previous question touched on the differences between how others see you and how you see yourself. This question reverses the discrepancy—others can only see the "you" of the survival system, but you sense that within you there is someone still waiting to be freed. The image to keep in mind is that of a butterfly unable to emerge from a cocoon and having everyone assume it is just a funny-looking twig.

*Are there parts of me that feel as if
they do not belong to me?*

Here we are looking at survival systems that were responses to the demands of another or vibrations of someone else's unmet dreams. Sometimes the demands are obvious, more often they are obscure and hidden. Parents' acceptance and love of their child can be based on how well the child responds to these silent messages.

Examples in this category include the son who pursues a career in baseball because his father dreamt of being a professional player or the surgeon who longed to be a songwriter but was following the family's tradition of medicine.

A realistic evaluation of your inherent characteristics allows for a more meaningful understanding of how you may have experienced your early environment and why you feel the way you do about yourself. Of particular value is evaluating the "goodness/poorness-of-fit" between your personality and your parents' personality. For example, if the stories about you as a child always relate to your so-called "dangerous" escapades and you now realize that your parents struggled with anxiety, you have an insight into why you have believed that you are "difficult."

Do I know the difference between a
habit and a survival need?

A habit is an acquired pattern of behavior resulting from frequent repetition. A behavioral pattern associated with a survival need is also frequently repeated but its roots go deeper than mere repetition. Let's say you have a habit of being late. Your friends complain that they always have to wait for you; your grades are lowered because you don't turn in your papers on time, or you get charged for a late check. You realize that you are paying an unnecessary price for an old habit; and since it is under your control, you begin to take steps to be or do things on time. But if you are chronically late because you have a need to lose credibility, then your changing will be blocked since it is not under your control.

Am I unhappy with how I relate to others?

If your answer to this question is "yes," you may have needed protection against a world that was intrusive, smothering, or filled with anger. The barrier built can be an invisible wall allowing the child to see and be seen, but not touched or able to touch others. Remember Len, the man who didn't know the difference between intrusion and involvement. He had an invisible wall that kept him from being able to feel a true connection to people. There are a number of variations of protective walls including:

> ▸ the need to remain apart from others;

> ▸ feeling threatened if another gets too close;

> ▸ having difficulty staying tuned into conversations;

> ▸ having others complain that you are not available or interested in them; or

> ▸ being seen by others as insincere, unreliable, or slippery.

Do I dislike the way others treat me?

How you are treated as an adult may represent the "echoes" of your past, reverberating in your present life. The term "echo" signals that someone is experiencing and/or repeating a pattern, as an adult, that was originally established in an earlier stage of life. Jackie's story is a good example of this. Jackie was caught in the "echo" of her not being able to say "no" at work because, as a child, she had had no permission to say "no" to the needs of her mother and siblings. And being a major participant in the myth of mother's being able to hear, Jackie later got caught in the myth of her brother's non-existent business acumen.

The "echoes" of your past, reverberating in your present life, can act as major clues as to why you may have needed a survival system. Pay attention to what doesn't feel right in your current life. It can be issues in your personal life, your business dealings, social interactions, or any activities with which you are involved. Look for consistent patterns, such ones in which you are:

> ▸ being ignored,

> ▸ being burdened,

> ▸ unfairly criticized,

> ▸ taken advantage of,

> ▸ called upon to rescue,

▶ expected to be perfect,

▶ expected to make everyone happy,

▶ expected to sacrifice for another,

▶ made to feel stupid,

▶ not respected,

▶ not trusted,

▶ being at the end of a yo-yo, and so on.

Then analyze these patterns to see if they have any connection to how and what you were subjected to as a child. If you do catch an echo, follow it to its source.

*Do I seem to lose a part of me when I am
interacting with certain people?*

A loss of confidence or a discrepant behavior when interacting with certain people can be a signal that you may be reacting to a vibration from someone or a situation that is triggering your system. Such reactions can include:

▶ feelings of anxiety,

▶ feeling overwhelmed,

▶ feeling small and insignificant,

▶ stammering,

▶ not being able to think or speak coherently,

▶ sudden rapid or breathless speech,

▶ unexpected yawning, sleepiness, and a drop in energy.

Use your new awareness of these reactions to better understand what covert messages are being sent or what danger you fear. The less time that passes between your awareness of your reaction and your recognition of what is happening, the more power you will have to change the interaction.

Take another look in the mirror and remember: the face and body that looks back is the physical "you"—your sense of "who" resides in that face and body is the psychological "you." To move toward changing, you must keep these reflections undistorted.

Step 4. A Look at Your Childhood Environment

The environment of your childhood is the physical, psychological, and sociological matrix into which you were born. It includes the observable external world encompassing such variables as: geographical location; your parents' physical and psychological health; their physical and/or emotional availability and patterns of addiction; your family's ethnic or racial background, socio-economic class, and financial stability. Also included among external factors is birth order, number of siblings, not having any siblings, and the presence or absence of significant relatives.

Childhood environments also include that which is nonverbal and non-observable—the implicit knowledge of how to be in that environment—what I call the "vibrations" of an environment. These covert messages are hidden within family interactions and remain unrecognized, either by the person sending the message or the one receiving it. An example of an environmental vibration would be the narcissism of Snow White's stepmother and her need to be the fairest of them all, resonating as a vibration of danger.

The following questions ask you to look at your early environment in a way that could explain why you, as an adult, seem unable to change that which you strive to change. To answer some of the questions, you may need to become a detective, looking at clues found in half-truths, distortions, and hidden dynamics.

Was my childhood a war zone? If yes, did
I build a tank? Disappear?

Environments that do not respect a child's integrity and boundaries can be imagined as a war zone. Certainly, any child subjected to physical, sexual, emotional, or verbal abuse is living in one, as are children caught in the battles between the adults in their lives. I also classify parents' addictions as a version of a war zone because of the chaos and uncertainty created by the out-of-control nature of addiction.

Characteristics associated with living in a tank can include, among others: an aura of being untouchable; inflexibility in both body- and spoken language; a strong tendency to "run over" ideas and people; and disparaging remarks acting as a "first strike."

For those caught in being invisible, a clue is the consistency of being overlooked, not remembered, or any experience of not being recognized. Behaviors that are consistent with your avoiding being the appropriate object of attention or focus are worth analyzing for their adaptive meaning.

Are there well-guarded secrets in my family that
would have required a survival adaptation?

Family histories that demand secrecy are, by definition, damaging environments. Secrets, such as a grandfather's suicide, father not being able to read English, mother's prescription drug addiction, or father's extramarital affairs, create a conspiracy of silence. Sometimes the child knows the secret, sometimes not. In either case, the secret is attached to a negative and/or punitive belief system that sends a signal that something or someone is "bad."

One of the consequences of maintaining family secrets is that they reinforce a sense of shame that is often the underlying reason for the existence of secrets in the first place. As mentioned, shame relates to feelings of inadequacy and self-contempt by an individual, a family, or a group. It's not about what one has done but rather what one is or is not regarding issues of character and acceptance by others. Secrets that are particularly powerful are ones that create fear and stress associated with the consequences of the secret being revealed, often resulting in an individual turning into a "silent child."

Ask yourself: Have I ignored vibrations in my family that might be covering unspoken secrets? Are there unexplained gaps and subtle distortions in the way my family history is told and questions family members seem to ignore or avoid answering? Was I a silent child and do I still feel restrictions on my ability to speak freely? When asked, do others experience me as too formal, withdrawn, or lacking spontaneity? Are there discrepancies between what my family insists was the reality of their existence and what I, now an adult, would recognize as being factually impossible?

> *Was there "an elephant in the parlor" that the*
> *family pretended was the family cat?*

Both family myths and family secrets distort a child's reality. But the very nature of secrets and the unspoken hidden messages surrounding them make them easier to unmask. Myths, because they become woven into the fabric of the child's life—not as a secret but as a distortion—tend to be accepted as real and thus ignored and overlooked.

As exemplified by Jackie, who was caught in the myth that her mother was capable of hearing, a family establishes a myth to deflect some aspect or characteristic of a family member that the individual member, in collusion with the family, experiences as dysfunctional or defective and therefore not to be acknowledged. This perceived negative characteristic is then denied by being wrapped in a myth of nonexistence.

As with teasing out family secrets, you need to ask questions that would establish the true reality of your family.

*Did my environment require that I
become a pseudo-adult child?*

By "pseudo-adult child" I mean a child who prematurely assumes the responsibilities of an adult in an environment in which the parent(s) do not act as adults. Both Beth and Jackie are examples of this. The child who becomes a pseudo-adult child usually appears, as an adult, to be an individual who is in total control of his or her life and expects and is expected to be responsible for the lives of others. But prematurely assuming the responsibilities of adulthood turns "maturity" into "seriousness" and increases the chance that adulthood feels like a burden. A different way of asking this same question would be: Do I feel burdened by all the responsibilities I carry? Ask yourself as well if you are caught in the trap of perfectionism, place unreasonable demands and expectations on yourself, and/or lack permission to play. If your answers are "yes," you may be caught in having needed to be a pseudo-adult child. It is time now to give yourself permission to give yourself back some of the freedom of childhood.

*Do I know of any special circumstances that
would have negatively affected the lives of my
parents, either as children or as adults?*

In trying to understand your own environment, it is crucial to understand the world from which your parents came.

Your system of survival is inexorably tied to what "hits" they experienced in their world, both as children and adults, and what they had to "duck," leading to their belief of what they needed to do in order to survive. Special circumstances, particularly when one or both of your parents were children, can include: experiences relating to war or political oppression; loss of a parent or significant parental figure; physical, emotional, or sexual abuse; dislocations and constant moving; economic disasters; and any event that would radically alter an individual's life.

All the forces responsible for your need to develop a survival system are also applicable to your parents and their parents. These vibrations, at times going back several generations, had the power to have affected you. The more you recognize them, understand them, deal with them, and free yourself from them, the less likely they will affect your children.

Were my parents caught in their own survival
systems and how might that have affected me?

Depending on their own history, personality, and life experiences, parents bring to the interactions with their children their own hidden beliefs of what they needed to be (or not be) that once met their childhood survival requirements. James, responding to the survival beliefs internalized by his father in the concentration camp, is an example of this.

Other examples include the parent who "needs to be needed" and the parent who "needs to control." The former is an individual who may have responded to being unimportant or unwanted as a child by establishing importance based on what he or she does for another. The controlling parent's stranglehold of power can serve a number of dysfunctional parental needs including: not being able to separate from the child, needing to be the one and only authority, and his or her own anxieties about being abandoned.

Was I caught in a good-parent/bad-parent dynamic?

Good-parent/bad-parent is where one parent is seen as the difficult one, the one who caused the problems. The other parent is the "good" one, the understanding parent. At first, the survival system appears to be a response to the parent who was difficult, demanding, or dysfunctional. But the real power of the need to adapt rests in the child's response to the good parent's need to pacify his or her spouse. "Don't upset your mother, you know how much she loves you," or "Be sure to agree with your father, you know how angry he can get," are phrases often used. Len, who didn't know the difference between intrusion and involvement, represents the child pressured to passively accept the inappropriate behaviors of the difficult parent to not only avoid a negative reaction from that parent but, more importantly, to not lose the approval and love of the perceived good parent.

Was I caught in destructive competition?

The environmental demand to avoid a competitive situation can be played out in many ways, including needing to be unattractive, needing to be dumb, needing to be unsuccessful, needing to be unmotivated, needing to not take anything seriously, or conversely, needing not to be taken seriously. This is an environment that sends a message that winning is all—in any way one can and at any cost to another. Excessive teasing, "innocent" jokes, cutting remarks, or lying to gain an advantage can be hidden signals of destructive competition. The competition can be limited to two specific members of a family or it can be a pattern of family dynamics going back several generations. Diane's aunt may have been specifically competitive with Diane's mother, and the competition played out through their children. It is also possible that the aunt came from a family that, for some unknown reason, got caught in destructive competition through several generations. Also watch for no-win situations that are symptomatic of family competitiveness.

> *Were there environmental demands by*
> *family members, other than parents?*

Grandparents, siblings, aunts, uncles, and cousins can play a role in a child needing a survival system. Certainly Diane's extended family members were key players in her "need to be stupid." Mark's grandmother, who was forever having a near-death experience, was another demanding family member. Other examples may include: a troubled older sibling who intimidates a younger child, an uncle caught in a scandal that drains the family's energy and resources, and cousins who are aggressively competitive. In exploring your history, include all of the people who played a part in that history.

Step 5. A Look at the Interaction

These questions explore the goodness- versus poorness-of-fit between you and the world of your childhood. Just to remind you, a goodness-of-fit will not need or result in a survival system. When, however, there is a negative discrepancy and/or conflict between the individuality of the child and the child's environment, the poorness-of-fit can result in a need for an adaptive system.

> *Do I have a sense of the "fit" between my*
> *personality and the personalities of my parents?*

To answer this question, look for the existence—or absence—of conflicts in current interactions between your basic personality and emotional nature and that of your parents. Since these characteristics tend to remain stable over time, who you are and who your parents are now, can act as a guide as to the nature of the fit when you were a child. Stories about you as a child can also offer clues to this question. Were you seen as too sensitive, perhaps too active? How about not friendly enough or too stubborn or too independent?

Was there a poorness-of-fit between myself and the
cultural practices and beliefs of my family?

A disparity can arise in situations where a family continues to identify with the practices and beliefs of its primary group and the child—now involved in school and new socializing situations—connects to the values, language, and practices of a more mainstream group. The congruence between the child, increasingly integrated into a new culture, and the static nature of the family group becomes increasingly strained.

Also check the fit between you and the larger world in which you existed. Ask yourself if you felt that you belonged in that world or were you someone who existed outside its boundaries.

Were there conflicts between my personality and
the parenting styles of my parents?

As discussed in the chapter on "The Interaction," some discrepancies between your basic nature and how you were parented are particularly damaging, and consequently more apt to result in a survival system. To mention just a few: a risk-taking child being raised by anxious parents; an anxious child dealing with angry, punitive parents; or a stubborn child with controlling parents. I encourage you to review those mentioned to see whether you and your parents were caught in a "fit" of incompatibility. And bear in mind that the message parents often send in such cases is that something is "wrong" with the child, rather than in the congruence between them.

Am I stuck in a chronic negative interaction
with one or both parents?

A chronic negative interaction is often tied to issues of control between the parent and the child, even as the child becomes an adult. I try to capture the power of such an interaction by asking a patient to try the following exercise. Extend each arm out to the side, with your right arm acting the part that is in control. Right arm says, "up." Left arm goes down. Right arm says "in." Left arm stays out. Right arm says "down." Left arm goes up. Which arm is in control? As long as the left only acts in opposition to the commands of the right, it is still caught in a controlling situation. The object is to free the left arm so that it evaluates the reasons for a movement and experiences true choice.

Step 6. A Look at Wrong Assumptions

By now you have a good idea of what fuels a need for a survival system, what is required to uncover one, and the hidden function it may have served. The next questions are posed to help you avoid incorrect assumptions.

Is a particular pattern of behavior always associated
with a particular environmental demand?

Seemingly different behaviors may be meeting the same environmental demand. There have been several examples cited in the various case histories.

For example, maintaining an unmarried state can be achieved by remaining unavailable. And remaining unavailable can be accomplished through a number of behaviors including acting as the perennial spinster, the playboy, and the dutiful daughter.

All will maintain an unmarried state even though each plays out different behavioral patterns. Regardless of the pattern, the childhood message from one or both parents would have been: "You must remain available to me."

Another example is the demand for one member of a family to acquiesce to the competitive needs of another. The survival systems that emerge will be reflections of whatever is caught in the destructive competition. Thus, there could be a "need to be ugly" or a "need to be stupid" or a "need to be a failure." Again, regardless of the surface pattern, the underlying reason represents your need to lose the competition.

Is my survival system a response to one, and
only one, environmental vibration?

Your childhood environment encompassed many factors, including your parents' external and internal worlds, family secrets and myths, hidden agendas, the needs and demands of the other, and such variables as birth order, siblings, and the presence or absence of other family members. Any one of these factors has the power to emit vibrations requiring a survival adaptation. If more than one factor is involved, your adaptation will respond accordingly.

Do I know who or what had the power in my family?

The power structure in a family is often obvious and usually rests with one or more adults. There are, however, some situations that are particularly difficult and confusing for a child. Let's say you have grown up in an alcoholic family, with father being the drinker. Who then had the power?

Most people answering this question say "the father." But he doesn't have real power because he cannot control his drinking. The family? They don't have it because they are caught in the powerlessness of the father's drinking. The power rests in the bottle, in the addiction. And power vested in a vacuum of power can be a key reason for a survival adaptation. I make this point because other conditions that create uncertainty or chaos can be substituted for the alcohol.

Are my parents necessarily "bad guys?"

The answer is no, for many parents have been unknowing participants in their own survival systems. Others have reacted directly and negatively to their own difficult environments. And some conveyed to their child the kind of world they believed their child needed to survive. Even if there is considerable evidence that a parent was abusive and destructive, it is crucial to stay free of the "my parent is a bad guy" syndrome. Continuing to blame them continues to give them enormous power that, in reality, they no longer have.

Step 7. A Look at Resistance

Imagine this! Our Snow White has uncovered her "need to be ugly" and begins to understand the how and why of her persistent, self-defeating behaviors. But instead of feeling relief, she becomes depressed and disappointed. She had assumed that, with an understanding of her survival system, she would automatically change and be free. However, confusion, frustration, and anxiety are more common responses to the initial understanding of one's system.

Is it really safe to change?

What if there is a piece of the "magic mirror" still left?

What if the "witch" hasn't lost her power?

What if my therapist and/or friends are
wrong and I'm still in danger?

Using Snow White as an example, she, like most people caught in a survival system, will feel that changing her system presents a great danger. Although intellectually she understands her survival system, emotionally she is still caught in the belief that she must remain ugly. Intellectual understanding is not sufficient to change a system; it represents the crucial beginning of an opportunity to change. It is essential that Snow White's continued resistance to change be seen as a continuation of the power of her survival system.

There is another silent "what if" hidden in a system. *What if I try to become beautiful and discover that I really am ugly?* Having internalized survival system beliefs and behaviors at an early age, Snow White has no real sense of her innate potential. Her survival system "persona" is the person she presents in the space-between herself and the others in her world, with responses from them in keeping with who she appears to be—thus reinforcing the "person" who lives in the survival system. Another perceived risk then, when attempting to develop what is a hope of innate potential, is the fear that the potential does not really exist.

Do I feel stuck and can I identify how
I maintain my stuckness?

The manifestation of a survival system is the "yes-but" syndrome. The person caught in such a system first says, "yes" to suggestions for achieving the desired change. There is a pause—followed by a "but"—followed by reasons for non-action. "Yes, I need to exercise—but—I really have so little time." "Yes, it is important that I get to meetings on time—but—traffic is so bad these days." This pattern of rejecting all suggestions from family, friends, teachers, and associates not only maintains the status quo, it often leads to a person struggling to break free of a survival system being seen as uncooperative, lazy, insincere, superficial, unreasonable, and lacking in discipline.

Another way unchangeability is maintained is by behaviors associated with such words as confused, ignorant, forgetful, and chaotic. Let's use "forgetful" this time as an example. One of the consistent themes of this book is the value of getting information about your history, your parents' history, and any other variable that might have played a part in affecting your environment. You begin to gather that information but somehow forget where you stored it and can't seem to remember the details clearly enough to draw any conclusion.

Here's another example. Imagination and imagery are powerful tools in achieving success. Think of the pole-vaulter who practices the high jump in the imagination of his mind. Can you imagine your changing to achieve your goals? Not being able to even imagine change is a strong indication of a resistance to change.

Take a moment now to ask yourself if you have taken the time to understand, analyze, and answer all of the previous questions. If you have not, is this a sign of the power of your survival system to resist your changing?

Step 8. Another Look at Some Techniques for Change

It may be helpful to review some of the suggested techniques for change.

Inductive/Deductive Reasoning

As you have read, a survival system is based on what a child believed was "The Truth." But what was "The Truth" in childhood can become the driving power of the adult's adaptive system. Using a concept from Formal Logic called a syllogism, we can see how, when used correctly, a syllogism acts as a formula for being able to draw valid conclusions from *known facts*. Made up of two statements, or premises, *both are assumed to be true*. The key to whether the conclusion is valid is based on the relationship of the two premises. Called deductive reasoning, the formula for being able to arrive at a valid conclusion is:

a = b (basic premise)
c = a (premise #2)
Therefore: c = b (valid conclusion)

I used a syllogism often learned in school as an example:

All men (a) are mortal (b) (a = b)
Socrates (c) is a man (a) (c = a)
Therefore Socrates (c) is mortal (b) (c = b)
If I had said that: All men (a) are mortal (b)
Socrates (c) is mortal (b)
Therefore Socrates (c) is a man (a)

You would correctly object. Just because Socrates is mortal, one cannot necessarily conclude that he is a man. Socrates could be a dog or any other creature that is mortal.

Remember, a syllogism can lead to a valid conclusion from known facts and in this case, the syllogism is invalid but the basic premises remain true.

The truth of the basic premise is established through observation. In the above examples, because we observe that all men who have ever lived have died, we conclude that: "All men are mortal." This is called inductive reasoning. Individuals gather information about their specific worlds and establish basic premises through inductive reasoning. They behave, once a basic premise is set, as if it were universally true. The validity of a conclusion may be questioned, but the truth of the basic premise is rarely challenged.

These hidden false premises from which conclusions are derived are important dimensions of an individual's internalized sense of reality and fuel a childhood need for a survival system. Thus an awareness of your internalized sense of reality becomes particularly important when dealing with a system. Questioning the truth of your basic premises offers great hope for change. If "all people are unreliable," you will have a difficult time establishing a secure relationship. If "some people are unreliable," then you stand a chance of finding someone you can trust. What are the false premises of your childhood?

The Space-Between

As discussed earlier, in the theater, the "space-between" refers to the kind of reality the actors are creating in any given scene. When a scene is not conveying the playwright's intent, the director attempts to change the "feel" of that space. Although the director may seem to be working with an individual actor, his focus is on helping that actor change what is being played out. The closer the actors get to conveying the meaning of the play in the "space-between" the more the audience will experience the reality the writer had intended.

Each time you interact with another, a "space-between" is created. The more you become aware of the kind of reality you and the other(s) are creating, the more the distortions in that reality can come to the surface. And the more you catch the distortions in the "space-between," the more power you have to create a different reality. As one of the actors, you must be aware of what you are putting into the "space-between."

As the audience, you must recognize the reality that is being created. If that reality is not what you want or intend to create, you may: (a) unknowingly be creating a false or distorted reality; or (b) you may have a clue as to what the other person might be putting into that space. As the director, you work toward creating the kind of reality you want. In some cases it is important to recognize that the "play" is heading toward failure and that, after much redirection of yourself, you may ultimately need to do some recasting of "actors."

For example, imagine you have an old friend, one who goes back to early high school days. You become aware that, in the last several years, times spent with her can sometimes leave you feeling upset, sad, and slightly angry. You begin to notice that you do not experience this reaction when you and your friend are together alone—only when there are others present. You start to focus on what is happening in the "space-between" and slowly realize that your friend is putting into the "space-between" the two of you and the others, a message of her greater importance and expertise. "Echo!" you say to yourself, recognizing the echo of the relationship you had with your older sister who always played the role of "The Older Sister." You also begin to realize that you have been a party to this interaction by your withdrawing into the shadows in order to not challenge or upset your friend. You have a choice of either confronting her or changing what you put into the "space-between" that will ultimately change the dynamics between the two of you.

The Value of Metaphor

As a tool for change, metaphors, fables, and stories that act as metaphors have powers to convey special meanings based on imaginative and natural associations between one experience and another, between one psychological state and another.

The Snow White versions effectively act as a metaphor for explaining a need for a survival system. Once established, any subsequent mention of a "Snow White need" allows for a full and clear understanding of the entire complexity of the survival system approach without further explanations. We have seen in Peter's case how references to childhood as a "war zone," and his "tank" allowed him to more fully understand his need for protection against his father's attacks. Another metaphor is the image of mousetraps holding ping-pong balls acting as a symbol for those chronic, negative interactions that can trap two people. The story of Emily captures this dynamic.

Although not mentioned in the case histories, I also use the fable of *The Emperor's New Clothes* as a metaphor. Some children, based on their personalities, emotionality, and high mirror neuron systems, are particularly sensitive and empathetic. They are more vulnerable to resonating to the vibrations in their environments and are children who, like the child in the story of *The Emperor's New Clothes*, sense that their emperors are naked. I turn the emperor's story into a metaphor to explain why children may need to deny their own reality in order to survive. Like all fables, there is a happy ending, with the child being honored. In reality, it is the messenger that is often in danger of being killed. Imagine how thrilled the emperor would be to have a child point out that he is standing nude in front of his subjects, that his advisors have lied to him, and that he has been severely conned. Survival would require that the child deny his recognition of the true reality.

The Use and Misuse of Words

Another source of information as to a distorted, internalized reality is found in the use—and misuse—of words. That kind of reality was at the core of Len's need for a protective glass wall; for if there is no difference between intrusion and involvement, protection is required. Review these pairs of words that can act as a clue to a need for a survival system:

- involvement and intrusion,

- deserving and indulging,

- caring for oneself and being selfish,

- successful and exploitive,

- healthy ego and narcissism,

- responsibility and burden,

- proud and vain,

- shyness and snobbishness,

- sensitive and weak,

- neat and compulsive,

- friendly and wanting something,

- confident and egotistical,

- assertive and aggressive,

- to need and to be needy,

- life is a process and life is a burden.

No-Win Strategy

A no-win strategy is a practical way of resolving problems or dilemmas that offer no positive solutions. You will be defeated whenever you attempt to find an answer that you think is a "win" when only a lose/lose result is possible and inevitable. The classic comic example is when your mother gives you two new shirts for your birthday. To please her, you immediately put on one of the shirts and she accusingly says, "Don't you like the other one?" No-wins can be great fodder for comedians, and often are; but they set up an individual to feel responsible for wounding another or, conversely, being wounded by the other. Mother expresses anger and disappointment that you didn't appreciate what she gave you, and you feel guilty that somehow you did something wrong and treated her badly. Any survival system in response to no-win environments is thus maintained as long as the individual continues to try to find a winning solution.

The four steps to minimize a no-win situation:

- The first step is the recognition that you are caught in a lose/lose situation, meaning that each of the choices offers more of a loss than a win.

- The second step is giving up the belief that one can win and that there must be some way of teasing out a winning choice.

- The third step is the understanding that whatever you attempt to do will elicit some negative result or reaction.

- The final step is to make a list of what is the loss and resulting reaction involved in each of the choices. The decision then of what to do is based on which choice offers the lesser of the two or more losses.

One of the positive results of this strategy is that the recognition that one is making a choice, even if it is of choosing the lesser of two losses, reinforces a sense of internal power.

Photographs

Photographs can be valuable clues to the past. How family members relate to each other can open doors of new information. Do they touch, not touch, touch inappropriately, look in the same direction, stand apart, include or exclude certain members?

Photographs of an individual as a young child often capture the essential essence of that person before environmental demands have taken their toll.

Secondary Adaptive Responses

Secondary adaptive responses are symptoms that emerge when an individual is caught in an inner conflict between the primary need of an original survival system and the increasingly important need to break free. Diane's story is a good example of this reaction. If you remember, Diane had originally sought help for her poor sense of self and bouts of depression. In the course of this therapy, she had uncovered her childhood history, understood her reactions to the difficult events of her childhood, and had made a number of important changes in her life. Several years later, she returned to therapy, now struggling with panic attacks which seemed to have no connection to her present reality. During these sessions, she recognized that beneath the behaviors and feelings associated with the traumas of her childhood, she had also been caught in a survival system. Her system effectively prevented her from hearing or recognizing when another person was demeaning or unfairly critical of her. Tracing the onset of the attacks and their current occurrences, she was able to recognize that her bouts of high anxiety were acting as an effective barrier against her experiencing and expressing anger at her employer and some of her associates who treated her with condescension and disdain. As long as she did not hear the remarks or acknowledge their negative edge, she was—according to her survival system—safe in her non-reaction.

Diane's recognition that an anxiety attack was a signal that she was being exposed to a demeaning interaction offered her an innovative method of negating her secondary adaptive response as well as further dismantling her system. Turning her negative experience of anxiety into a positive one, Diane began to use anxiety as a signal that someone was putting her down. Over time, she was able to quickly convert the anxiety cue to an action and object to the negative comment.

Anxiety or panic attacks are particularly effective as secondary adaptive responses. The emotional intensity associated with them can block or mute other reactions or emotions that would reveal behaviors that a system would consider "dangerous." Any physical or emotional response that short-circuits movement out of a system can act as a secondary adaptive response. These can include: crying, instead of being able to speak; twitches or tics that cause a shift in attention; sudden feelings of intense shame; and experiencing confusion for no apparent reason. The experience of being able to use what normally would be considered a dysfunctional response in a positive way enhances a sense of inner power.

Step 9. A Look at Your Changing

We come now to the ultimate question:

How can I make change happen?

Your understanding and appreciation of the original purpose of your survival adaptation will not automatically free you. Breaking free requires that you re-evaluate your beliefs and basic premises, attempt new behaviors and experiences, and risk the power of the magic wand.

Children who have needed to develop survival systems often do not develop a capacity to be alone—a capacity that develops when a child is allowed to be alone in the presence of a supportive "someone." It may be valuable for you to examine this idea as it relates to your life. And equally important would be for you to develop positive, supportive "someones" who could offer you a sense of "presence." In this regard, a trusting relationship with a therapist can be a valuable asset.

Change Starts Here. Change Starts Now.

Make the unknown knowable, talk to your parents about their lives and backgrounds and encourage family members and childhood friends to share what life was like when you were growing up.

Look through your family photo albums and notice the way people relate to each other. Ask yourself, do they touch, not touch, touch inappropriately, look in the same direction, stand apart, include or exclude certain members?

Find a picture of yourself as a child that reflects your true inner self. Enlarge it, frame it and place it within easy view. View this picture as representing your potential, your inherent aliveness, and your hidden self.

Wander through memories of your childhood and note the discrepancies between the "you" of your family and the "you" of the outside world. Imagine yourself and the people in your life as if they were characters in a movie. How does the plot play? Do the characters seem to be real? Who are the heroes, heroines, and villains? Is it a mystery, comedy, tragedy, or war picture? And what role have you been cast to play?

Recognize the possibility that your parents may have internalized a trauma and educate yourself about it. Talk to people who have experienced the same or similar traumas and look for other sources of information such as books, films, and lectures.

Break the negative hold of long-buried secrets by sharing them with close friends. Exposing secrets lessens their power and takes them out of the realm of being "unspeakable."

Unwrap a family myth by evaluating whether it is a denial of reality (e.g., mother is just a "funny" lady—actually she's dysfunctional and a threat to the children) or a distortion of reality (e.g., we come from royal stock—actually we come from parents who served royalty).

Form your beliefs into syllogisms and look for false premises that have influenced your feelings and behaviors. Analyze not only the validity of your conclusions but, most importantly, the truth of your premises.

Review the list of words given in Chapter Eleven and check a dictionary for the meaning of any words that you may be misusing. Become aware of how you use, or misuse, language.

Counter the "yes-but" syndrome by using it against itself. Become conscious of how often you say "yes-but" and then find ways to articulate the problem in a positive way, countering the negative with a positive. Listen for the "yes-buts" in the language of the people around you.

Check out the "shoulds" and "should-nots" of your childhood and explore your reaction to them. There will be major adaptive differences between compliance to authority and a universal "no" to all authority. The latter traps you into saying "no" to all suggestions, even ones you are giving to yourself.

Tap into your interests and creativity to develop them as a special kind of understanding. Many stories, fables, and images can be used as metaphors for various aspects of survival systems.

Recognize when you are caught in a no-win situation—when there is only a lose/lose solution. Make a list of what is involved in each loss and then decide which choice offers the lesser loss.

Avoid the "nuclear reactions" of your interactions and understand what ping-pong balls your mousetrap may be holding. Try to understand what ping-pong balls the other person may have in his or her mousetrap and how each of you sets off the other. Find a way of signaling that the mousetraps have been set off and take a "timeout" before the explosion.

Involve yourself in activities that allow for greater flexibility and enjoyment and consider new challenges such as dancing, acting, joining a chorus, or learning to play a musical instrument. If you lost the chance to be a child during your childhood, allow yourself time now to make up that loss.

Reclaim Your Power

Your success in reaching the light side of your moon will be blocked as long as you continue to believe that someone else holds the power and that *they* must first change before you can be free.

> *The key that unlocks a survival system is your recognition that only one power matters: The power you already possess to change yourself.*

With an acceptance and embracing of this basic premise comes the recognition that you have been an unknowing participant in the perpetuation of your survival system. You will also begin to realize that there is a part of you that clings to old beliefs and behaviors, not only because they signify safety, but also because they are the only ones you have known. What then emerges from this recognition is a growing conflict between the two separate parts of yourself—the "you" of your potential who wants to break free, and the "you" of your survival system that refuses to risk change. Each part will fight for control of your life.

*The challenge you now face is: Which "you" is
going to be in control of the rest of your life?*

Do not underestimate the force of the conflict. A survival system is deeply ingrained and does not willingly relinquish its power. But the conflict can be won when the supportive adult part of you can treat the resistant part—the part that belongs to your childhood, the part that had needed a survival system—with kindness, tolerance, understanding, and patience.

Do not expect the journey of discovering your full potential to be quick and easy. As you have read, a survival system based on childhood beliefs of survival has strong roots, deeply ingrained. It does not easily give up its power. But the journey is well worth taking; for at its end will be the recovery of your inner life, your authenticity, and the freedom to be who you truly are.

A number of years ago, a patient gave me a framed copy of a wonderful quote. I hung it on the wall in an inconspicuous place; and when someone reaches the threshold of breaking free, I point out the words:

*"And the day came when the risk to remain tight in a bud
was more painful than the risk it took to blossom."*

—ANAÏS NIN

In the process of breaking free, that "day" can extend over a long period of time. As mentioned throughout this book, a child's creative survival adaptation does not give up its power easily or willingly. How long it takes one to "blossom" depends on the reason, nature and degree of the original adaptation, and the demands of the current environment. What is important is that you continue to explore dynamic ways of breaking free. You will not only find your hidden potential, you may also affect the childhoods of your children.

Welcome to the light side of your moon.

Appendix

Review of Questions Asked

General Questions

You know what you want but you can't seem to get it. Could it be you have a hidden need to not get what you want?

Is it possible that you are caught in a survival system and that, as a child, you had to develop a hidden need to not get what you want?

Whose needs did get met?

If you had a magic wand and could make your wants a reality, what would change?

Would there be any danger to you, or to someone else, if the magic worked?

Are there negative consequences to breaking free from your survival system?

How does a child get the hidden messages of the inner world of the parent?

It can be helpful to imagine that you are a character in a movie: How does the plot play? Do the characters seem authentic? Who plays the roles of hero, heroine, or villain? Is the movie a mystery, comedy, tragedy, or war picture? In what "role" have you been cast?

Has your system prevented you from reaching your potential by consistently stifling or negating physical, social, or intellectual opportunities?

Do you overreact to a seemingly benign memory?

Do you not react to a recalled event and wonder if your lack of reaction is appropriate?

Do you find it difficult, demoralizing, or strangely unnerving to be alone?

Breaking Free from a Survival System
Do I need, for some unknown reason, to_____?

Step 1: A Look at Your Present Life

Is there a discrepancy between what I want and what I am able to get?

Is there a discrepancy between who I think I am and who I want to be?

Is there a discrepancy between what I have wanted to be or do and what others believe I should do?

Do I feel that I'm living only half a life?

Do I long to be free of some unknown burden I carry?

Do I continue to behave in ways that defeat my goals?

Are there clear signs or signals that point to the existence of a hidden survival system?

Step 2: A Look at the Danger

Am I clear about the principles and theory of Darwinian survival as it relates to me?

Do I understand the power of attachment?

Do I understand how children think, feel, and experience their world?

Do I understand the concepts of the "good-enough mother" and "whose needs got met?"

Is there a discrepancy between what I want and what I am able to get?

Step 3: A Look at You

When I look in a mirror, is the reflection of my physical image positive or negative?

How should I describe my personality and emotional nature?

Is my impression of "me" different from the impression others have of me?

Do I feel that there is a different "me" waiting to be free?

Are there parts of "me" that feel as if they do not belong to me?

Am I unhappy with how I relate to others?

Do I dislike how others treat me?

Do I seem to lose a part of "me" when I am interacting with certain people?

Step 4: A Look at My Childhood Environment

Was my childhood a war zone? If yes, did I build a tank? Disappear?

Are there well-guarded secrets in my family that would have required a survival adaptation?

Have I ignored "vibrations" in my family that might be covering unspoken secrets?

Was there "an elephant in the parlor" that the family pretended was the family cat?

Did my environment require that I become a pseudo-adult child?

Do I feel burdened by all the responsibilities I carry?

Do I know of any special circumstances that would have negatively affected the lives of my parents, either as children or as adults?

Were my parents caught in their own survival systems and how might it have affected me?

Was I caught in a good-parent/bad-parent dynamic?

Was I caught in destructive competition?

Were there environmental demands by family members, other than parents?

Step 5: A Look at the Interaction

Do I have a sense of the "fit" between my personality and the personalities of my parents?

Was there a poorness-of-fit between myself and the cultural practices and beliefs of my family?

Were there conflicts between my personality and the parenting styles of my parents?

Am I stuck in a chronic negative interaction with one or both parents?

Step 6: A Look at Wrong Assumptions

Is a particular pattern of behavior always associated with a particular environmental demand?

Is my survival system a response to one, and only one, environmental vibration?

Do I know who or what had the power in my family?

Are my parents necessarily "bad guys?"

Step 7: A Look at Resistance

Is it really safe to change?

What if there is a piece of the "magic mirror" still left?

What if the "witch" hasn't lost her power?

What if my therapist and/or friends are wrong and I'm still in danger?

What if I try to become beautiful and discover that I really am ugly?

Do I feel stuck and can I identify how I maintain my stuckness?

Have I taken the time to understand, analyze, and answer all of the previous questions?

Another Look at Some Techniques for Change
Inductive/Deductive Reasoning

The Space Between

The Value of Metaphor

The Use and Misuse of Words

No-Win Strategy

Photographs

Secondary Adaptive Responses

Step 9: A Look at Your Changing
How can I make change happen?

Which "you" is going to be in control of the rest of your life?

BIBLIOGRAPHY

Bates, J.E., Wachs, R.D., and Emde, R.N., (1994) Toward practical uses for biological concepts of temperament. In J.E. Bates and T.D. Wachs (Eds.) *Temperament: Individual Differences at the Interface of Biology and Behavior.* Washington, D.C.: American Psychological Association.

Danieli, Y., Rodley, N.S., and Weisaeth, L., (1996) Introduction In Y. Danieli, N.S. Rodley and L. Weisaeth (Eds.) *International Responses to Traumatic Stress.* Amityville: Baywood Publishing Co., Inc.

Darwin, Charles R., (1859) *On the Origin of Species by Means of Natural Selection, or, the Preservation of Favoured Races in the Struggle for Life.* London: John Murray.

Figley, C.R. (1983) Catastrophies: An overview of family reactions. In C.R. Figley and H.R. McCubbus (Eds.) *Stress and the Family: Volume II: Coping with Catastrophe.* New York: Brunner/Mazel.

Fonagy, Peter (2001) *Attachment Theory and Psychoanalysis.* New York: Other Press.

Goldman, D. (1993) *In Search of the Real: The Origins and Originality of D.W. Winnicott.* London: Jason Aronson, Inc.

Jones, Steve (1999) *Darwin's Ghost: The Origin of Species Updated.* New York: Ballantine Books.

Kohnstamm, G.A. Bates, J.E., and Rothbart, M.K. (Eds.) (1989) *Temperament in Childhood.* New York: Wiley Press.

Marris, P. (1991) The social construction of uncertainty. In C.M. Parkes, J. Stevenson-Hinde and P. Marris (Eds.) *Attachment Across the Life Cycle*. New York: Routledge.

Siegel, Daniel J. (2007) *The Mindful Brain: Reflections and Attunement in the Cultivation of Well-Being*. New York: W.W. Norton.

Siegel, Daniel J. (1999) *The Developing Mind: How Relationships and the Brain Interact to Shape Who We Are*, New York: The Guilford Press.

Spiegelman, A. (1986) Part I: My Father Bleeds History, Part II: And Here My Troubles Began. In *Maus: A Survivor's Tale*. New York: Pantheon Books.

Scharf, M. and Mayseless, O. (2011) Disorganizing Experiences in Second- and Third- Generation Holocaust Survivors Qualitative Health Research Vol. 21.

Stern, Daniel N. (2004) *The Present Moment in Psychotherapy and Everyday Life*. New York: W.W. Norton & Company.

Thomas, A., and Chess, S. (1999) *Goodness of Fit: Clinical Applications from Infancy through Adult Life*. Philadelphia: Brunner/Mazel.

Winnicott, D.W. (1971) *Playing and Reality*. London: Routledge.

Winnicott, D.W. (1958) The capacity to be alone. In *The Maturational Process and the Facilitating Environment*. London: Hogarth.

ABOUT THE AUTHOR

Ditta M. Oliker, a clinical psychologist, has been in private practice in Los Angeles for thirty years.

Her first career was in theater, starting at the University of California, Los Angeles. UCLA had recently formed a partnership with members of the film industry to establish a professional theater on campus known as *The Theater Group*. The organization evolved into the Mark Taper Forum at the Los Angeles Music Center, with Oliker as a member of the core producing staff.

After a personal tragedy, she went back to school where she received her PhD. She began to develop her ideas about psychological survival and the lasting effects of the experiences and hidden messages of childhood while in graduate school. She continued to develop these themes after beginning her practice and incorporated them into her innovative concept of *Survival Systems*. Dr. Oliker has lectured on the subject at various universities and mental health facilities, including UCLA and Alliant University, among others.

Her innovative approach to the field of psychotherapy is based on her knowledge of psychodynamic theory interwoven with her theater background. Her concept of survival systems is based, not only on theory, but also on her understanding of the struggles of her patients; on her own life history; and on her work in the theater, which showed her the power of creative communication.

Dr. Oliker's popular blog, *"The Long Reach of Childhood,"* is featured on www.psychologytoday.com. For information about seminars, presentations, or professional consultations, email dmoliker@aol.com.

INDEX